THE COMMONSENSE BOOK
OF A COUNTRYWOMAN

The Commonsense Book of a Countrywoman

Hannah Hauxwell

ISIS
LARGE PRINT
Oxford and Orlando

Copyright © Hannah Hauxwell and Barry Cockcroft 1999

First published in Great Britain 1999
by Great Northern

Published in Large Print 2000 by ISIS Publishing Ltd,
7 Centremead, Osney Mead, Oxford OX2 0ES, and
ISIS Publishing, PO Box 195758,
Winter Springs, Florida 32719-5758, USA
by arrangement with Great Northern

British Library Cataloguing in Publication Data
Hauxwell, Hannah, 1926-
   The commonsense book of a countrywoman. – Large print ed.
   1. Hauxwell, Hannah, 1926- 2. Country life – England –
   Yorkshire Dales 3. Common sense 4. Large type books
   I. Title
   942.8'4'082'092

ISBN 0-7531-5775-6 (hb)
ISBN 0-7531-5778-0 (pb)

Printed and bound by Antony Rowe, Chippenham and Reading

To Lydia, my beloved mother

CONTENTS

INTRODUCTION

By Barry Cockcroft

Less than twenty minutes into that first meeting in a partly abandoned Yorkshire dale on a cold July day in 1972, I knew I had a programme.

What I did not realise at the time that it was the start of a cottage industry.

Fifteen television documentaries, constant media attention and this, the seventh book, across twenty-seven years (as I write) and still the Hannah Hauxwell saga rolls on. Gone, thankfully, is the frenzy of those early days when police had to be called to clear crowds blocking the road outside the bookshop where she was appearing and middle-aged ladies tottered out gasping "I touched her" . . . when it was more practical for the GPO to deliver the Hannah mail direct to my desk at Yorkshire Television — in sacks . . . when life was lived in a constant state of disbelief.

I lost sleep, believing I had ruined this poor lady's life. Nothing like it had happened before . . . or since. Thankfully, she insists she has relished it all.

Now matters proceed at a stately pace, as befits a maiden lady of a certain age. That flood of mail has declined to a steady stream, the demands of the media have moderated, publishers no longer demand a book a year, and the waiting lists at public libraries have dwindled.

But a walk down any street in this nation turns into a marathon. I have known twenty minutes become two hours. For she is a celebrity (a status she stoutly denies, by the way) of a different kind. The people she meets unexpectedly in the street do not react as though they have touched a high voltage cable, as in the case of film stars and other demi-Gods, but approach her as if meeting a very dear friend. They beam with delight, respectfully form queues to exchange a few words, obtain an autograph and be photographed with her (no flash, if you please!). She becomes a prisoner of her own fame, but even when time is pressing she remains a model of courtesy.

One question they always ask — are there more programmes and books in the pipeline? Which is why, after a literary silence of six years, this book came about. Television offers are awaited!

Hannah's appeal is international. She reaches across cultural, social and language barriers. Scandinavia, Australia, New Zealand and Canada have all fallen under her spell following the appearance of the programmes and books. It would be interesting to see the reaction in those countries if she ever visited. In the meantime, they turn up on her doorstep, sometimes by the coachload.

She also has an uncanny ability to become the focus of attention in places where she is totally unknown. Some nerve is touched, and waiters, hotel porters, receptionists, assistant managers and train guards spring to her side, offering assistance and greetings.

It happened throughout a six week tour of the United States, where only one person recognised her yet she was treated like minor royalty. None of the major networks have shown any interest in her programmes, the only exposure confined to local public broadcast systems with tiny audiences.

One PBS executive did join the multitude of admirers when he visited London for a sales convention and was offered a Hannah series. Normally, they dip into shows for a matter of minutes but he sat through three solid hours. When someone expressed surprise, he murmured dreamily: "She reminds me of the grandmother I never had!"

At the other end of the scale, I have seen sturdy hill farmers with weather-beaten faces and hands like shovels — an uncompromising breed in all circumstances — waiting in line to meet Hannah, red of face, twisting their flat caps into knots and sometimes too overcome to speak. It says much for the lady that she is so admired by her own folk.

So . . . what is it about Hannah Hauxwell? How does she reach so many people? Obviously, it has something to do with the innocence that shines from her. But she is an icon, an inspirational force capable of moving people to tears so there must be something else. I know one fact for certain — she has not changed her personality and attitude to life in any way since I first met her all those years ago. Fame, adulation just wash over her. She hardly notices it.

I once overheard a journalist who had just finished an interview say to the next in line: "Watch out for the aura." I knew exactly what he meant. There is a definite atmosphere around her, often aided by a shaft of light, whether from the sun or a lamp, which backlights her finely spun white hair. And she has a luminescent smile.

Nature itself seems to smile on her, conspiring to aid that remarkable image. For that first film I hoped for snow in November to underline the hardship of her life. I got a blizzard and a sunset. When, in the final sequence of the last major documentary many years later — perhaps the most poignant of them all since it chronicled her agonising departure from Low Birk Hatt — and the furniture van with her possessions had to be dragged out of the snow by a powerful tractor, it happened again. A glorious sunset ignited the entire scene.

One very senior television executive, not noted for dispensing praise, was moved to call it the shot of the year.

All I ever did was point the camera.

A Misfit at the Mirror

I have always felt something of a misfit . . . perhaps still do to a certain extent. Outside the home I didn't have a happy childhood, didn't like school and found it difficult to make friends. I felt rather left out, like the ugly duckling in the Hans Christian Andersen story.

But then one day I looked in a mirror and discovered to my surprise that I wasn't really ugly after all. In fact, I was reasonably pretty. I was about nine or ten at the time, and it was the first occasion I had looked at myself in a mirror in that way.

Up to then I had assumed that I was very unattractive, indeed, and my experiences at the little school in Baldersdale seemed to confirm that. I wasn't popular with one teacher, who was a good woman in her way but should never have been a teacher. She had her favourites, and whilst that is no crime she shouldn't have shown it. Now she didn't actually say I was ugly but she certainly gave me that impression, telling me I waddled like a duck, for instance.

No, I didn't like school at all. I even played truant one day, during lambing time. I disappeared up into the hills. Mother found out, of course, and she was cross with me. But she didn't smack me. I don't recall her ever smacking me. But that teacher did. She caned me across the palm of my hands once or twice — I don't know what for. But to be fair to her I have to say she didn't hit very hard.

She was the Sunday School teacher as well, and there was one very embarrassing incident when I was one of a group to be presented with a bible for good attendance. All the others turned up with a basket of harvest gifts, but I had nothing to offer. No-one had told me or my mother that was the tradition. I felt so strange standing in line with the others, empty handed. It was dreadful. The moment still comes back to haunt me. And it wasn't as if the Hauxwells weren't generous in these matters. My grandparents gave to the church. Grandad sent produce from his lovely garden and Grandma gave a quilt she had made herself to a sale of work.

I was so glad when I reached the age of fourteen and could leave school. In fact, for quite a considerable time — not regularly, but now and again — I would have nightmares that I was still at school. And when I woke up, it was such a lovely relief . . .

Even today I still regard myself as something of a misfit. Some people have asked whether I would have been happier had I been born in a different age and situation, even imagining me like a character out of a Jane Austen novel indulging in polite conversation, sewing, playing the piano and attending Regimental balls! It's a nice thought, but I don't think I would have fitted in anywhere.

Apart from one or two exceptions, I suppose I have been happy with the time and place in which I was born.

Bernard Raw was the most likeable boy in Baldersdale School, and I am pleased to still be his friend. He left the dale to live in Darlington, where he met his wife, Rene. They now reside in Scarborough and I meet them regularly in June at the Combined Services Reunion in Bridlington. A dance is held on the Saturday, followed by a beautiful service the day after when ex-servicemen and women parade with their flags.

Keeping the Germans at Bay in Baldersdale

I have something of a guilty feeling about the last war, because we were so very fortunate compared to most people. Farm prices went up and we were given subsidies, which made such a difference particularly when you consider that the Depression only just preceded the war and that had been a terrible time for farmers.

People in the towns and cities were being bombed and food was not plentiful. We were issued ration books like everyone else, and we also had a pig to kill at the given season and other homegrown produce, so nobody went hungry in our family — or anyone else in Baldersdale, for that matter. It must be said that war made life significantly better for hill farmers, generally. A sad thought, really.

We had a local air raid warden who arrived and ordered us to black out our windows should the Luftwaffe decide to target Baldersdale. I recall that we had a stable lamp — the sort that gives out a grand light — and it was decreed that the top half of that should be painted out. He also instructed that bicycle lamps should be similarly covered. During the Battle of Britain, at least one enemy plane flew over the dale and we knew about one being shot down somewhere. We heard later that there were others brought down in the Teesdale area but we never knew about it at the time.

The peace of Baldersdale was disturbed — but by our own side. Tanks came to practise across the water from us — Blackton reservoir, that is — and you could still see the tracks they made in recent times. Public transport became something of a problem in the dale. A bus did come occasionally to our side, but not to the other. So one old friend who farmed on the deprived side decided to buy a car. Because she had never had one before, this created a real bureaucratic pantomime about why she should need it, and whether she qualified for a petrol ration. They sent forms with such daft questions that she eventually declined to fill them in. She told me: "I were sick of 'em, so I wrote 'em a letter saying that if they wanted to know they mun come and see for themselves — that there was nowt but military up our side".

Another feature of wartime caution concerned the reservoirs in Baldersdale. They had high walls and big iron gates which they decided to keep locked against the enemy. I never could work out what kind of deterrent that would constitute but it created a problem for me when I went out on my bicycle because I couldn't lift it over the gate to get to the road. Fortunately, there was a small gate further along which I could manage. It meant you had to cross private land but the owners were kind enough to allow people to use it because of the circumstances.

They also placed a man on guard down Hury reservoir bank, but I don't know if they had a rifle to spare for him, or not.

The Laurel and Hardy Episode

The locking of the iron gate did lead to one incident which brought a bit of light relief to the dale during the war years, and is still remembered.

In those days, there was a small place called Blackton House — since demolished — which was occupied by water board workers and situated behind the gate. One day in the summer, the brother-in-law of one of the water board men turned up to visit him. He was from the West Riding of Yorkshire, engaged in the boot and shoe business, I believe, and a jolly good-natured soul. And what a big man he was, too. From his chins downwards he looked like a big jelly. He was accompanied by a friend, who was small and thin — physically the exact opposite. Together, the pair must have resembled Laurel and Hardy, and turned out to be just as comical in their way.

They had arrived at the gate by taxi from Cotherstone where they had clearly taken refreshment, and I don't mean a pot of tea! When they established that the gate was locked, a real argy-bargy ensued. It was heard by a friend of mine who was haymaking in a nearby field at the time, and later told the tale well.

The thin man was urging his friend to 'tek a running jump at it, and throw thissen o'er'! The large one was protesting loudly that he was unable to comply. Having seen him myself on one occasion I can confirm that he certainly wasn't built for the task.

The noise they made was eventually heard in Blackton House and the brother-in-law was summoned to the scene. When he realised the circumstances he returned not only with the key to the gate but a jug of black coffee to help them complete their journey!

When I was young and daft, I would regularly walk from Low Birk Hatt to Cotherstone. It was roughly six miles. I'm still daft, but no longer young.

Wartime Visitors . . . Evacuees and Soldiers

Early on in the war, a group of young evacuees came to Baldersdale from the North East — mainly Newcastle, Gateshead and Sunderland, which were targeted by the Luftwaffe in a serious way. A fairly large number were accommodated initially along with two of their teachers. But quite a few didn't stay long. I suppose they were homesick — it must have been a culture shock to arrive in the wide open spaces of a quiet Yorkshire dale after living in the crowded, noisy streets of a big town or city. Mind, they would have been well looked after with plenty of good, wholesome food to eat — probably more than they could expect back home. The lady teacher who arrived with them returned as well. But three of them went to the other extreme and stayed in Baldersdale when the war ended, so they must have taken to country life.

They were billeted around the local farms and those remaining, maybe about twenty in number, attended our school. The teacher who stayed with them taught them and some of the older Dales scholars, including me. But not for long, because I made up fourteen in the summer of 1940 and didn't stay a moment longer than necessary!

As far as I remember, there wasn't much integration between the evacuees and the local youngsters, apart from a little fraternisation at playtimes and dinner times. They were a fairly tough lot and one or two scraps happened between the boys, which was inevitable under the circumstances. One of our school bullies got his comeuppance as a result.

Two of the smaller visitors took a shine to me. They were brothers called Bobby and Johnny, and canny little chaps they were, too. Johnny, the younger one, would come to me to ask to have his coat fastened.

Cotherstone, the village just outside Baldersdale where I now live, also gave shelter during the war — to the military. I understand some of the poor boys had been through the ordeal of the Dunkirk evacuation. The local chapel was used to accommodate one group, and later in the war we even had some Italian prisoners of war billeted locally.

The British boys joined in the social life of the village and it was at one dance that I met that fair-haired soldier I mentioned in one of my earlier books. He was playing in the band and asked me to stay until he finished. But that didn't prove possible because I wasn't allowed to stay out late.

I never saw him again, and often wonder if he survived the war.

The Gooseberry Bush Telegraph and Other Forms of Communication

During the war and for some years afterwards, there was only one telephone in Baldersdale. It was situated in Reservoir House, near to Hury reservoir lower down the dale where the Water Board official, Mr Tunstall, resided. It constituted the only swift method of communicating with the outside world in the event of accidents, sudden illness or other emergencies.

And on one notable occasion, to announce the arrival of a flock of chickens — with the assistance of a gooseberry bush!

High Birk Hatt Farm, just above my place, was the home of the Thwaites family and Miss Violet Thwaites had married a relative of Mr Tunstall and set up home at Lanquitts Farm, down the dale from Reservoir House, but visible from there on a clear day. Violet and her mother, Mrs Thwaites, had ordered some chickens to be delivered from suppliers outside Baldersdale and then worked out a system of communication to let them know when the chickens were on their way. It was arranged that the suppliers would ring Mr Tunstall, who kindly agreed to signal the fact to Violet by placing a white tablecloth on a gooseberry bush in his garden. This was quite an urgent matter for young chickens can be very vulnerable and their welfare a high priority. It may have been a comical method of communication, but apparently it worked.

One other traditional means of spreading essential information in Baldersdale was via the postman. We had some colourful characters in the old days who took on many unofficial extra responsibilities, such as delivering newspapers — particularly the *Darlington and Stockton Times*, which everyone seemed to read, on Saturdays — accepting outgoing letters and taking messages to Reservoir House if, for instance, a doctor was needed. People used to look forward to the postman calling because he knew what was going on in the area. I remember one called Johnny Alderson, who had a good sense of humour and was a dream for people seeking information about local events and personalities. I know he had a lot of fun over the gooseberry bush affair. I think he was the son of a Cotherstone cobbler, and I knew he served in the air force during its early days, possibly during the First World War.

The first postman I knew was another lovely man called Cecil Coulthard. I felt sorry for him because he didn't have good health and all he had to transport him round the dale was a bicycle. The strain of delivering mail in all weathers must have taken its toll because he left to go to Darlington. Later on the Post Office provided a van for Baldersdale, which would have made his life so much easier.

We had another droll stick, Tom Ireland, who came from Upper Teesdale and had a habit of addressing his lady customers as "honey". He landed at our house one winter Saturday when there was a bit of snow about, and saying: "Oh, man ... I've got to go now to Blackton and Start House with letters and newspapers. Hast thou an old hoss I can borrow, honey!" Now he had fought in the First World War and had been gassed. I don't think he lived to be an old man.

I heard another story about his dry humour, which happened when he was on relief duty in Lunedale. A woman on his round had reported him for some trivial, so-called offence. A little later he got his own back. Postmen weren't obliged to accept letters to go, but usually did so in the Yorkshire Dales because postboxes were often a long walk away. Anyway, Tom met this woman coming towards him with a letter to post, but he carried on by saying: "Put it int' postbox, honey. I'll git it t'morn!"

Grandma Hauxwell did say once that some people never had a good postman, but we never had a bad one.

If I had one wish, it would be that my mother could have experienced some of the privileges I am enjoying now. She had to work so hard, and had so much worry.

Learning to Love the Telephone

The telephone and I were strangers for many years. Following the war quite a few farms had one installed and the one readily available to me was at the Youth Hostel in Baldersdale.

But I had precious little use for it until I began my television career. From time to time, Barry Cockcroft would need to speak to me to make arrangements for more filming, and he also phoned during really bad winter weather to make sure I was all right. Being all on my own, you see . . . he was worried that I might slip and fall and nobody would know.

Setting up a conversation meant a lot of to-ing and fro-ing between Low Birk Hatt and the hostel, which was a burden on Richard Megson, the Warden. But he was very good about it. At first I wasn't at all comfortable with the telephone. Didn't even like to handle the thing. Richard was very understanding and would kindly make the call, and then hold it to my ear until I got the hang of it. Barry said you would have thought it was a cobra, poised to strike!

Now, of course, I have one of my own and it has become one of life's essentials. Barry will confirm that I am now one of British Telecom's best customers.

I met a walker once on the Pennine Way, which ran through my land, and he asked how far it was to Middleton-in-Teesdale. I said it was about six miles, or maybe five as the crow flies.

He replied that he was no crow!

From Balderhead Reservoir . . . to the Mediterranean

Curious thing, I've always been fascinated by ships but didn't like water as a child — rather afraid of it, in fact. And there is a great deal of water in Baldersdale, since it is home to four reservoirs, Blackton, Hury, Balderhead and a subsidiary. I understand water comes all the way to Baldersdale from Lunedale, sometimes at a bit of a rush. I recall years ago when I was a girl we had relatives living at Briscoe, across the water ground. To get there we had to cross a bridge over a bywash, where the water runs down swiftly from one reservoir to another. That always made me nervous. There was nothing wrong with the bridge. It was just me.

Mother liked the sea. But the few times we were there together on day trips I never ventured on a boat. She did once, on a visit to the East Coast. But not me.

Oddly enough, the water ground in Baldersdale became my fairyland during the long years when I was living on my own at Low Birk Hatt farm. I used to gain solace from its beauty, listening to the sound of Hunderbeck running into the Balder and watching the moonlight reflecting from the surface.

But I never learned to swim, nor had any particular fancy to do so. I know it's a healthy exercise and all children are taught these days but there were no swimming lessons at Baldersdale School. There was nowhere to learn then, except the reservoirs and they were far too dangerous. You had mud near the edges and strong currents because of the constant movement of water down the various levels. A lot of things young people take for granted today just weren't thought about years ago.

The first time I ever went aboard a boat was in the 1960s. And it was on the newly opened Balderhead reservoir. An alderman came to perform the official ceremony and local people were invited to an Open Day. They were offering boat trips, and by that time I had grown out of my childhood fear of water. So I went afloat for the very first time in my life on a small boat with a little engine. It passed off without incident so I gained enough confidence to take the ferry between North and South Shields in the company of some friends in the North East. I suppose that must count as my first sea voyage.

It was not to be the last!

I suppose you could say I went from one extreme to the other . . . From a cockleshell on Balderhead to the grandest ship afloat.

The QE2.

Three times now I have been privileged to travel on the very last of a special breed of vessel, a super liner capable of crossing oceans at a steady thirty miles an hour. And constructed by British shipbuilders, another special breed which, unfortunately, is also virtually extinct. I recall Captain Burton-Hall, the master of the QE2 on my first voyage (to New York), telling me it was not financially possible to build such a quality ship these days.

The first thing that struck me about the QE2 was its size. It is so enormous that when you board at Southampton you cannot get a view of the whole of the ship — just part of it. Even in New York I couldn't see it all. And I sailed with her all round the Mediterranean and still didn't find the opportunity to appreciate it fully. Indeed, it was on my third trip when we docked in Oslo that I was able to get high enough and far enough away to see the ship to its best advantage. It was silhouetted against a blue sky — such a magnificent sight.

I prefer my transport on the slower side, such as boats . . . so it will be no surprise to learn that I have an affection for steam traction engines as a result of attending, on several occasions, the annual Elstronwick Steam Rally, held near Hull. For ten years, it was organised by Ken and Molly Floater, who have become my good friends. It all took place in one field over the weekend, and has raised a lot of money for charities. They put up a big tent and held a concert on the Saturday evening, featuring a splendid piano accordion band, plus one violinist. Those steam engines come in all sizes, and I had a ride on one which was only a few feet from the ground. Along with Molly, I also tried to ride a three-wheeled cycle. But it had a mind of its own and I couldn't get anywhere with it!

The Anniversary Cruise . . . Parties, Caged Birds and a Brief Encounter with Sir James Savile

The second time I was kindly invited aboard the QE2 was a very special event — the 25th anniversary cruise. As we left Southampton bound for the Mediterranean, there were bands playing, streamers floating down the decks to the dockside and excited people waving as tugs pulled us slowly away from shore. Such a sense of occasion . . . quite unforgettable.

Having sailed to New York with the QE2 on the opening leg of my tour of the United States for the television series, "Hannah USA", I knew what to expect when I was escorted to my cabin. Really, it was more like an hotel suite because the ship was built in the days when designers were generous with space. That is such an important consideration, because I feel that space equals grace. Even the bathroom was larger than some London hotels provide. I have heard about people who have travelled regularly on the QE2 switching for a change to one of the recently built cruise ships and finding that space is somewhat at a premium. One gentleman in particular, who could afford to cruise every year, wrote to one of his friends on the anniversary cruise about this problem. A generously proportioned person, it seems, he said that his bathroom on the new ship was so small he could scarcely move in it. He added that he was never going to "jump ship" from the QE2 in the future!

Speaking of friends, I had an old shipmate to see on this cruise. We met on my voyage to New York when she noticed that the ship's librarian, June Applebee, and myself were somewhat under pressure during the first of my book signings. There was a very large queue, and she kindly came to our assistance. When we finally managed to finish, we shared a pot of tea and became firm friends. Joanne Wall is a very energetic American lady from Pittsburgh, and grandmother to numerous young people. Since we met, she had even published a book of her own, dedicated to the grandchildren on whom she dotes. We kept in touch after parting in New York and I was very pleased when she wrote to tell me that she, too, had booked on the anniversary trip. We were to share many pleasant hours during the next eight days.

Do you know, I once met a lady journalist who told me that she had been bored whilst travelling on the QE2. Maybe she was trying to be clever, or blasé, but there is no hope for someone who really thinks that. Believe me, there just isn't time to be bored on the QE2. You are on the go from morning 'til night, with parties, dancing, theatre shows, excursions ashore and exceptional meals. And it you fancied some exercise on board, it is just a mile walk along the main deck, which winds all the way round the ship. Or you could attend the gymnasium, which is one amenity I confess I avoided.

As for me, I also had my duties to attend to so my time was really full. On the third day I was asked to sign books again and, since it was the actual day that the QE2 set sail on her maiden voyage twenty-five years ago on May 2nd, 1969, I felt quite honoured. Despite the efficient organisation of the library staff and the help once again of Joanne, so many people turned up that I was kept busy for two hours. People naturally want to chat when they have gone to so much time and trouble — and expense — and I am not the swiftest of persons. I've heard that some famous authors (not that I place myself in that category) refuse all conversation during signing sessions to maximise sales, but I cannot do that. It is the customer who is doing the author the favour, not the other way around, and they are entitled to courtesy and proper attention on these occasions.

The day after the signing we arrived in Palma, the capital of Majorca. The weather was glorious, and in the afternoon I went ashore with Joanne and an American gentleman called Bob.

As we left Palma harbour we passed an enormous American aircraft carrier, lying at anchor. I was told it carried more people than the QE2. Five thousand souls, which beat us by two thousand. That night I went to the Officers' cocktail party where I had my usual soft drink as everyone else downed champagne. I always say on those occasions that I don't touch alcohol because I'm daft enough sober! The senior officer asked me to sign the Special Visitors' Book, which I realised later was a great privilege because two of the other signatures were Elizabeth R and Philip.

The next port of call was probably the most enjoyable, except for one unhappy situation. Barcelona is a lovely place and its main attraction for me was the Rambla, a long and spacious tree-lined avenue running through the heart of the city all the way down to the harbour. Cars are allowed only on narrow roads on each side so pedestrians can wander down the middle in reasonable safety-up to a point. Cycles are allowed and some were ridden in a hazardous manner. I had a couple of scares. The Rambla has dozens of little shops and stalls, some displaying glorious arrays of flowers, and attractive squares off to the side where you could take tea in the sun. But the one disappointment in an otherwise memorable afternoon came when we found that among the flowers were rows of caged birds for sale. Such beautiful little creatures, with magnificently coloured plumage. It was a sad sight, and reminded me of the only time I had a real disagreement on my travels. That happened in Sienna, where they hold that violent horse race around the city square. It is common place for the poor animals to be injured, sometimes fatally. I voiced my disapproval to a waiter during lunch in the square and he argued strongly in favour of the race. I stood my ground, and in the end we agreed to differ and parted friends. But it has to be said that I consider some attitudes to animals on the Continent to be less than kind.

Anyway, I put all that behind me and returned to the ship to prepare for the most important event of the cruise

— for me, and a certain gentleman, that is. First, there was the Captain's cocktail party to attend, the most prestigious of the lot. Leaving my cabin for the party, I had the rare distinction of being picked up at one end of the corridor by Sir James Savile and then dropped within minutes at the other end! I had met Jimmy previously at a very lavish party at Clivedon, the Astor mansion which has a magnificent library particularly appreciated by Barry Cockcroft. The occasion was the 150th anniversary of the founding of Thomas Cook, a royal event attended by Princess Diana. We had got along famously then and it was good to see him again and be swept along towards the Captain's party by such an effervescent personality, however briefly. He disappeared at the end of the corridor, whisked away by an admirer. Quite understandable, since everyone wants to meet Jimmy.

Immediately after the party came the testing time, when I would have to sing for my supper, so to speak. The early burden had to be shouldered by that certain gentleman I mentioned earlier — Barry Cockcroft. He is the man who arrived at my farm one July afternoon in 1972 and started a happy relationship which continues to this day. Up to now, he has made fifteen television programmes about me and helped to write half a dozen books. So, if you want to blame anyone for all the fuss, he's the one!

Together we have presented "An Evening With Hannah Hauxwell" on many occasions and in many different surroundings — hotels, libraries and even theatres. Even so, Barry always finds it rather nerve-wracking, saying he is more accustomed to being

23

behind the camera not up front. He says he is the warm-up man, going on stage first to tell the audience how we met, relating a few facts about my early background and then showing an extract from one of the documentaries before introducing me. A question and answer session between us follows until Barry judges the time is right to invite questions from the audience.

Thankfully, it all went well. More than that, in fact. The QE2 theatre is very large, but it was full that night. Indeed, several people were obliged to stand at the back. It was a very warm audience who asked a barrage of questions and when Barry had to call a halt for reasons of time we basked in the glow of a standing ovation.

The next stop was Gibraltar. The ship docked a distance away from the town and the queue for taxis was so slow that we — that is, Barry and his wife, Celia, and I — decided to walk. It was a long, hot and dusty trek and I was relieved to find a table at a café to relish a cup of tea whilst my more energetic companions went off to explore. They didn't have long because we had to leave in the early evening, bound for Lisbon, arriving next morning with the sun burning down. I delayed visiting the centre of the city until the afternoon so I could conserve some energy for a rather spectacular evening on board. Lisbon was our last port of call before heading home so to mark the occasion there was a series of events culminating in a midnight supper in the largest restaurant. It was an amazing sight, that supper. Some clever person or persons had carved dozens of ice sculptures, which were draped with the most exotic foods. Lobsters, oysters, smoked salmon, patés, cheeses, fruit, cakes and desserts. A veritable feast. But there was a problem. We had all dined so well not long before that all but a few trenchermen could only stand and admire, or nibble a little at the most. But it was not to be wasted. In the early hours I noticed that the delicacies hegan to disappear rather swiftly as crew members (not waiters) emerged from below decks to carry it away.

I was very happy for them. They deserved a treat because they all work so hard so that we can live, for a few golden days, like lords and ladies.

The Titanic Incident . . . and a Lost Passport

Dear Joanne did have a fright one day when she saw members of the QE2 crew donning lifejackets and assembling alongside the lifeboats. She thought it was a real crisis and hurried to find me and help me to abandon ship, Titanic-style! I suppose that is something of an exaggeration in the telling, but she was truly concerned. Of course, there was a simple explanation. It was just the crew going through the same emergency drill all the passengers have to do. They do it separately because they are busy helping us during our practice.

Mind, the poor lady did have a genuine crisis when we returned to Southampton — a double one, in fact. Not only did all her luggage vanish but she couldn't trace her passport. It took a long and stressful time before she was reunited with her possessions.

I was lucky to grow up among books, and with people who loved them. It opened doors.

The Bane of My Life

Prominently displayed at all my book signing sessions and other public appearances you will find a notice saying: "PLEASE . . . NO FLASH PHOTOGRAPHY!" On the QE2, Barry Cockcroft kindly took it upon himself to patrol the long queues waiting to have their books signed, searching out cameras and politely asking people not to use their flashlight. In the early days it did not bother me but now it causes great discomfort in both eyes. Even when I wear dark glasses and close my eyes I can still see redness. It has really become the bane of my life, since most of the people I meet on my travels want a photograph as a memento, and their cameras all seem to have an automatic flashlight!

Like Fats Waller, My Feets Too Big!

There is another problem which has been troubling me far longer than flash photography. Like the Fats Waller song says . . . my feets too big. Worse than that, even. They are also very broad and, to cap it all, one toe is bent underneath. It is possible that wearing Wellington boots for so many years on the farm may be responsible. But I'm inclined to think it may be more to do with the way they design footwear these days. To begin with, the sizes are all to pot. They confuse me with these new European measurements, but I think I used to be seven prior to the Common Market. And shoes now seem to be made, in varying degrees, to taper off just when I want them to stay wide. So I have either to get a pair a size bigger which makes them too long and clumsy, or do without. It's a nightmare. I have tried dozens of pairs on and the local shops have been very kind and patient in the struggle to find something suitable. I did find one practical solution at the Army and Navy Stores — a pair of boots with very wide toes. I've had them for years now, and they are close to falling apart. I intend to try and find another pair.

But . . . you cannot turn up for something like the Captain's cocktail party in army boots. I found a way round that predicament by wearing carpet slippers — but very smart, dark blue creations with an embroidered crest!

I am not good at finding my way about. On one notable occasion I got lost in the Kensington Hilton. I was in the dining room with a friend who had to leave, so I went to bid her farewell. I couldn't work out the way back to my table and after a considerable time I came across one of the hotel staff, who guided me along the correct route.

A Thousand and One Balloons . . . and a Cowbell in Oslo

There was another spectacular start to my next cruise on the QE2, bound for the capitals of Scandinavia. Bands were playing as usual as we set sail, but then they released a thousand and one balloons into the air, which floated high in the air over Southampton docks and away over the sea towards the Isle of Wight. It was done to celebrate the one thousand and first voyage of the big ship, and we were all presented with a certificate to commemorate our participation. I was also pleased to meet up once again with my companion from the New York and Mediterranean trips, Joanne Wall. We had kept in touch by letter and telephone and since she had always wanted to visit Scandinavia she booked herself a passage.

As usual, there was no chance to become bored because I had to go straight to a lunchtime cocktail party held for the entertainers. That's how they described us, but I wouldn't class myself as such. There were several celebrities present and I had the pleasure of meeting and talking to the singer, Edmund Hockridge. I recall most fondly his radio shows in years gone by. He told me he came to Britain during the war with the Royal Canadian Air Force. He was to be the star of the opening cabaret that very night, so he was the first to sing for his supper! Another major personality at the party was Mr Kilroy-Silk, a former Member of Parliament and now the host of a popular television chat show. He gave a fascinating talk about his experiences during the afternoon of the following day, spent at sea. So he was another one to discharge his responsibilities early on. I had to wait another four days for my turn.

The first port of call was Oslo, which I will always remember as a very special place, for more than one reason. To begin with it was blessed with lovely open spaces, and a series of wide and sweeping steps and lots of trees and greenery — always an essential for me. There were lots of impressive statues, too, so I imagine that Norway must have several celebrated sculptors. I walked all the way into the city centre with Barry and Celia Cockcroft, and Celia pointed out some of the places she had known as a young college student when she took a summer vacation job in Oslo one year.

And then Barry bought me a gift. Something he knew I really wanted. A cowbell! There's a story behind it, of course. I came close to acquiring a cowbell in Austria once, during my tour of Europe with Barry for the "Innocent Abroad" television series back in 1991. Trouble was, the shop offered many different sizes of cowbell. Now I have to admit that I am notoriously slow in making important decisions, and I pondered so long that I missed my chance. You see, we were at a border crossing and we had to suddenly leave. When you are negotiating more than a ton of film equipment through difficult and suspicious Customs officials, shopping for souvenirs ranks very low in the order of priorities. I was quite disappointed, because I had owned several cows in my farming days but none of them had bells! They have such a melodious tone, too, and possessing one would have reminded me of my lovely Rosa, the senior cow, and all her children. They were the nearest I had to a family for a number of years. Anyway, in the middle of Oslo, Barry was reminded of that occasion in Austria when he spotted a cowbell very similar to the one I missed. He didn't give me the opportunity to agonise over the choice this time, and had it bought and presented in double quick time!

We left Oslo in the late afternoon and sailed down the fiord towards Denmark. We had arrived the previous evening in darkness and rain so we had no idea how beautiful a classic Norwegian fiord could be until we left. It turned into a glorious evening — the beginning of a spell of unusually warm weather — and everyone on board was spellbound by the scenery. Unlike anywhere else in the world, I imagine, and the light remained constant until eleven thirty.

By the time we reached Copenhagen the sun was so hot that you could have believed that we had sailed by mistake to the Mediterranean. It may have been somewhat unseasonal, but no-one was complaining. The capital of Denmark did not seem quite so spacious to me as Oslo, but it did have one particularly appealing spot: the Tivoli Gardens. It was Barry Cockcroft this time who had previous knowledge of the city, having made a documentary about a Danish inventor early in his long career with Yorkshire Television, and he knew that the justly famous Gardens would be the place for me. We headed straight there and, indeed, spent most of our available time walking round and appreciating its beauty. The flowers, lakes, fountains and magnificent variety of trees dazzled the senses. We had refreshments at a café overlooking one lake which had an old fashioned galleon moored in the middle, which housed a restaurant. I wondered how they had managed to transport it there, since it was in the middle of a city.

We set sail at two in the morning for Stockholm and the weather deteriorated next day, which didn't matter a great deal since it was all spent at sea. I was summoned at noon to a book signing session, and the queue was as long as ever. Joanne helped, as usual, but it still took one and a half hours to clear.

Our arrival the following morning at the shores of Sweden generated a great deal of excitement because the QE2 chose to anchor off a small town called Nyasham. The locals had never seen a ship anywhere near that size before and came out in a flotilla of small boats to welcome us and gaze at the giant in their waters. The warm and sunny conditions we enjoyed in Denmark had also returned, so all was set for a splendid day. But not for me, alas. To begin with, I felt rather off colour. And then I realised that this was not a place where you could stroll ashore down a firm gangway. Instead, it was necessary to board one of a fleet of small boats and be ferried quite a distance to Nyasham harbour. Now I know I had conquered that childhood fear about going on a boat, but apart from feeling under par I was reminded vividly of an unnerving experience on a less than tranquil sea entering the Blue Grotto in Capri aboard a rowing boat. It was necessary to endure that for the sake of the television series, but it was something I would not repeat willingly. So I opted to stay on board, and spent most of the day in my cabin nursing a feverish kind of cold.

The rest of my party were taken by coach to Stockholm and came back with glowing reports of sunlit squares, outdoor cafés and a visit to the royal palace. And when they arrived back at Nyasham, they had been invited to the local Midsummer celebrations, a kind of country fair where they watched a display of Swedish folk dancing. I was sorry to miss that.

It was still hot enough in the late afternoon for people to swim and sunbathe in numbers. But the most memorable part of the day was yet to come. As the QE2 moved majestically away from shore, at least 80 boats poured out of Nyasham harbour and swarmed around us — everything from expensive motor cruisers to tiny yachts big enough for just one person. They were all calling and saying farewell. The ship's officers responded swiftly to this moving spectacle and organised a band to play for them, even finding a bagpiper to weigh in with what I imagine was a Scottish lament at having to leave such a friendly place. As we picked up speed, those who were capable did so, too, still waving and shouting. It was really exciting, carried on for ages until the superior pace of the QE2 left behind all but a couple of the speedboats and I think that most people on board were feeling quite emotional as the rest of the fleet became dots in our wake. Nature made its contribution, too, as a mother-of-pearl sky turned into a marvellous sunset. It was an experience to cherish, and all the better for being completely unexpected and spontaneous.

The next day dawned bright and sunny again, a factor which made both Barry and myself very apprehensive. You see, it was our turn to "perform", and instead of arranging it as usual for after dinner in the theatre it was decided to make it a mid-afternoon affair in the Grand Lounge. Which meant we had to compete with the lure of the sundeck and the swimming pool. Who, we reasoned, would forsake that to sit in a stuffy lounge and listen to a country bumpkin prattling on? To our immense relief, the place was crowded again, and the response of our audience matched the weather in its warmth. In fact, the cruise director came to tell us how surprised he had been at the turn-out and the way we had been received. He said that he had to mark all his "entertainers" out of five in his report to senior management, that he was going to give us top marks and would be glad to see us on another cruise. We did not demur!

He then hurried me off to yet another book signing, which gratifyingly lasted for an identical one and a half hours. I finished just in time to go on deck and witness the QE2 sailing by the new suspension bridge linking east and west Denmark, which was followed immediately by a very novel event. A Danish television programme had arranged to land a helicopter on the upper deck, which I understand was covered live. Everyone turned out to watch — at a sensible distance — as the helicopter pilot manoeuvred very slowly and safely to rest.

That excitement over, I just had time to get ready for the Captain's cocktail party. The day concluded with another of those amazing midnight buffets, again featuring large ice sculptures adorned with expensive delicacies. Which again few people could do justice to because we had all dined so well. They disappeared below decks, as before!

The last day of the cruise was also blessed with glorious weather and, since we were heading back home with no more landfalls, meant everyone could relax and recover on deck. There was a final party that night in the Officers' Mess, a farewell to another exhilarating voyage.

I suppose I'm what some people would call the worst kind of English person abroad when it comes to food. I eat only what I know I like.

Travel Ambitions . . . the Holy Land, Elephants, and Odette Country

When I talk in public about my travels, I am always asked if I would care to head off to foreign parts again, and if so, where. The answer to the first part of the question is a definite "Yes", but the second part is not so easy. There are many places on my list.

The Holy Land is near the top, Africa to see elephants in their natural habitat because I am so fond of them, back to America to try and find some real cowboys because my trip to Texas wasn't very successful in that respect — where they were hiding I've no idea — and as far as Britain is concerned I'm attracted by Scotland, which I haven't visited as much as I would like.

Most of all, perhaps, I would like to explore what I call Odette country. Those of you who lived through the last war will recall Odette Hallows, one of the great heroines of our time. A feature film and books celebrated her exploits as a Resistance fighter in France, for which she was awarded a medal for bravery.

When I attended the Women of the Year Lunch at the Savoy Hotel in 1977, I noticed on the invitation that

Odette was listed as a committee member. I asked if it was possible to meet her, and when all the ceremony and the speeches were over she came over to me. It was a great thrill. We talked, and she told me she had seen "Too Long A Winter". Her husband wrote to me afterwards to say she wasn't well. Sadly, she is now dead.

I would love to see the places where she operated in France, hunted by the Gestapo and taking such risks. Barry Cockcroft has done the research, identifying the key areas and would like to make a television documentary, following me on what would be a pilgrimage to honour the life of a truly great lady.

Another book I read recently reminded me very strongly of Odette's exploits. Written by a French colleague, it was the biography of Edith Cavell, the English nurse who in France during the First World War courageously helped British soldiers to freedom, just like Odette. She cared for anyone sick, whatever nationality, and she even nursed German wounded. But the Germans tried and executed her.

On my first visit to London, I was happy to chance upon her memorial outside St Martin's in the Field.

When I acquired the book about Odette, I had my hat and coat on and some washing on the line. I thought I would just look at some of the pictures. Several hours later I still had my hat and coat on and the washing was still on the line . . .

The Good Pig . . .
and Little Joss

My travels in later life meant experiencing a choice of foods which were inevitably unknown to a lass from Baldersdale. I got off to a flying start in Paris, the first foreign city I encountered, and from there ate my way through Germany, Austria and Italy. Occasionally, I had to inquire just what it was on my plate!

America was a different proposition altogether. The food was usually recognisable, but the individual portions were sufficient to feed an entire family. On one occasion in a New York diner, four of us ordered two dishes between us and it was still too much. Where possible, Barry Cockcroft sought Chinese restaurants during our six week tour of the United States, and I found their fare quite tasty.

But I have to confess that I am a heathen when it comes to food. A top class French restaurant might be wasted on me. My preference would be shepherd's pie followed by apple pie. And bacon and sausage are all time favourites. If there wasn't any other kind of meat, the good pig would keep me happy.

My family kept pigs, and the first two I remember as a child became my playmates. We always made pets of

39

our pigs, and once mother and I reared one on a bottle. Daddy must have been good at picking the right sort and rearing them properly because he won two cups at agricultural shows.

The last pig we had was really lovely, a little chap called Joss. He was the runt of the litter and we got him at the same time as a sow. She used to bully Joss, but even when he grew up into a big pig he was always friendly.

In the end, we had Joss for bacon. That was why we bought him. I made myself scarce, as usual, when the time came. It's said that farmers cannot afford to be sentimental about their animals. I was, of course, but I just had to accept it.

A Yard or Two Further . . .

I am often asked about the contrast between Low Birk Hatt in Baldersdale and Belle Vue Cottage in the village of Cotherstone, where I live now. Well, they are two extremes in more than one way. On the one hand, I now have water on tap, central heating and shops and people close by. On the other, I used to have none of those amenities but I had lots of space to myself and was a long way from the nearest road.

Now, if my house was moved a yard or two, I would be ON the road . . .

If I Could Pull Up Roots . . .

. . . the place I would probably choose would be Grange-over-Sands, a lovely little place on the edge of Morecambe Bay. I have made several really good friends in the area. And the sea attracts — after all, I did live by water for more than sixty years and do miss it.

The Music of the Trees

Another of the things I miss through living in a village is what I call the music of the trees. Quite a number grew near my old home, in the garden overlooking the reservoir and on the water ground near the iron gate.

They would often play for me. Not the howling of a winter storm, of course, but the lilt of a gentle westerly.

The Old Byre Is Now a Visitor Centre

They call them "The Hannah Hauxwell Meadows", which is quite an honour. When I put Low Birk Hatt up for sale — very reluctantly, but advancing years, bad winters and some niggling health problems forced the issue — the Durham Wildlife Trust bought the major portion of my pastures.

There were certain wild flowers, plants and grasses flourishing there which were apparently unique for miles around. My old-fashioned farming ways — no inorganic fertilisers, just the natural stuff, and no re-seeding except for the top pasture during wartime — had given them the opportunity to survive when all around them perished. But I have to admit that I wasn't aware at the time that I was being so ecologically kind. Such wonderful names they have, too, like meadow foxdale, crested dog's-tail, floating sweetgrass and the really attractive hay sward. That is blue, tinged with violet, and probably just as pleasing as the famous blue gentian of Upper Teesdale, mentioned in another part of this book.

Now they have even turned my old byre into a Visitor Centre. It was officially opened by Thelma Barlow, the

42

actress who played Mavis Wilton in *"Coronation Street"*. They did ask me to do it, but I never go back to Low Birk Hatt. It is still the place I love most, and to see it again may seriously unsettle me.

I was once asked if I had fallen into bad habits after leaving the farm, such as sleeping in. I replied that I hadn't, because I was always in the habit of sleeping in. I don't pretend that I've ever been a good riser.

Born Ahead of My Time

When I was obliged by circumstance to become a one woman farmer, local opinion by and large probably concluded that I wasn't very good at the job.

So isn't it remarkable that they are encouraging, even paying, people to do exactly what I did — or didn't do. Organic farming has become very desirable and the movement is led by no less than the heir to the throne himself, Prince Charles. I must say I do admire him, and not just for the agricultural methods he has pioneered and publicised at Highgrove and the farms under his control.

They even have this set-aside scheme, to persuade certain farmers to do nothing with their land for a while. I don't agree with the idea, but it would have been nice in poor farming years to just sit back and receive cheques from the bureaucrats.

I suppose I was born ahead of my time!

It's no secret that my financial position had improved, but I had to go carefully for most of my life and I still do. Once you have trod that narrow path, there is always fear. Security and independence are very important. Not that I value money for its own sake, but it is easy to get into a spending habit and end up with nothing when done.

Anyway, I'm a Yorkshirewoman!

Charlie, the Fat Man and Big Bruno

One day whilst going round Stokesley Show in the North East, a grand day out which I have enjoyed several times, I met an old friend of mine called Bruno. Of course, I made a fuss of him . . . and people became rather concerned for my safety.

You see, Bruno is a bull and a gentleman of large proportions. Around one and a half tons of beef on the hoof.

Now I'm well aware that bulls can be very dangerous, and statistics show that farm workers are injured and even killed most years by beasts not thought to be aggressive. But I have always got on well with bulls, and have known quite a few down the years.

As for Bruno, I had met and become friendly with him on a previous occasion, when friends took me to his owners, the Pye family of Middleton-on-Leven, near Yarm. He is a Saler, a French breed, and he has won prizes all over the place. I understand he was considered to be the best of his breed in the world. He is famous in several countries and his semen has been exported to the United States and beyond. Indeed, when my friends

Nancy and Fred Smith, the retired farmers who act as my hosts at Stokesley Show, went to New Zealand they discovered Bruno was known there, too. He is looked after by herdsman Jim Ridley, a real down-to-earth countryman, who kept an eye on the situation when I posed for photographs holding Bruno's rope.

We had bulls in Baldersdale, of course, and I cannot recall any of them being involved in unpleasant incidents. As children, we were taught to be cautious because even the quietest can suddenly turn nasty. The Friesian breed, for instance, is reputed to be unpredictable.

But all my own experiences with bulls have been happy. I borrowed bulls from friends in the dale, including one from Maurice Atkinson when he was farming Clove Lodge just across the water from Low Birk Hatt. His was a Hereford, a grand old chap I named The Fat Man. Then there was Charlie, the Charolais from Sleetburn, and he was nice, too. I used to fodder them along with my own cattle, wandering among them and nearly forgetting that one was a bull.

They sired some fine beasts. My Rosa, the senior cow when I left the farm, was a daughter of The Fat Man. As for Charlie, I got a bullock from him which topped the market at Middleton-in-Teesdale.

I was pretty proud of that, seeing I was supposed to be a woman who couldn't farm properly!

Rosa's teeth went, so that was the end of the line for her. But I did meet her again after I moved to Cotherstone. They held a fun weekend in the village and Bill Purves brought her down. I had mixed feelings about it, but I went to see her — and Rosa knew me, so I was glad I did.

All my cattle had names. Her Ladyship had daughters called Bumpkin and Whiskers, as well as Rosa. Then there was Septimus, who had a lovely temperament, and Patch, Puddles (sometimes called Bumble), Bunty and others. The last one I had was Mr Christmas, who arrived at the festive time.

The Hauxwell Patent Hay Piking System

My questionable farming skills were once referred to in a most flattering way by my good friend, Bill Purves, who was working Clove Lodge when I left Baldersdale. He featured in *Hannah's North Country*, the book Barry and I wrote in 1993, where he related how I had rescued some hay for him.

It was the last of the crop that year and the weather had been poor. Bill brought a baler to try and pick up the mown hay but gave up when the baler got stuck in the mud. In fact, he decided to abandon it.

Now Bill had done me a great favour one dry summer when he saw me toiling to and from the reservoir with a gallon can to collect water. I must have spent months, maybe years of my time at Low Birk Hatt fetching water like that. The film sequence most people talk about when they meet me is the one where I had to break the ice, then carry buckets for my thirsty cattle up the slope and through the snowdrifts. Remember, there was no water on tap at my place.

Anyway, when Bill spotted my predicament he filled a two hundred gallon bowser with drinking water, hauled it by tractor to my door, and left it. Such a good man. So when he gave up on that hay I saw my chance to do something for him in return. There was nothing really wrong with it — just a bit damp — so I set to raking and forking it by hand to improve it. I gave it a chance to dry a bit before returning to start piking it in the old-fashioned way, building up a conical shape to a height of about five feet. The trick is to keep the middle nicely stable, not setting it too high or it would slip. Topping off is the worst part of this method. It always takes me ages to shape it properly, narrowing it off but making sure the top was not too pointed, and then binding it closely to give it protection from the rain. Bill said my pike tops reminded him of thatching. There were two of them when I finished and Bill was kind enough to say that they made sweet hay for his beasts.

Haytime was my preferred time of the farming season, much more desirable than pig-killing, when I would make it my business to find work as far away from the scene as possible, and sheep shearing which we had to do by hand, of course. I was expected to help with that but I wasn't much good at it. The sheep were hot, sweaty and greasy and uncle would have to tie their legs and start the shearing for me — opening them out around the neck and stomach. It was not to my taste.

The main drawback to haytiming was usually the weather. We had some really tough times over the years. Piking it by hand was the system when uncle was alive. It was the practice to throw sacks over the pikes once they had settled a bit, and I did have a brainwave to improve matters. A sack doubled wasn't that effective

49

— they were the good-sized four stone variety — so I opened them out and prodded baling string through each corner. Then I put more string round the bottom of the pikes and placed the sacking on top, securing the four lengths of string to the lower one. It was necessary to keep a close eye on their progress because pikes generally drop, lose shape and cause the sacking to slip. I would go round and tighten everything up.

There was a bad spell during haytime the year uncle's health began to decline, and we had a lot of pikes to care for. I topped them all out with my own system, and it worked well.

One bad winter not long before I left Low Birk Hatt, I went three whole weeks without seeing anybody. And just under three weeks during a second, very lonely time.

The Tale of
Her Ladyship — My
Little White Cow

In the minds of many people, I am indelibly associated with a little white cow I called Her Ladyship. She was the only companion I had when the television cameras arrived at Low Birk Hatt in November, 1972, aside from the one calf she had each year which usually went to market to provide my main income.

And she was there in that debut shot in "Too Long A Winter", trailing behind me through a driving blizzard. Photographs of the two of us must have been published hundreds of times in newspapers and magazines.

People sometimes ask about her during the question and answer sessions with the audience at "Evenings With", and are always amused by the story of how I came by her.

When Uncle Tommy died three years after mother and I was left on my own, there was a sale of our stock. I kept one animal to farm on with, but she died so I started to look for another. Some friends in the dale who were rearing cattle for sale brought them up to my farm for summer and I spotted this little white heifer among them. A price was agreed, and over a cup of tea later I met a friend who was a cousin of the owner. As we were walking away together, she asked, "Are you buying that little heifer, then?" I replied that I was, so she said: "Aye, but it's a little 'un".

A little further on she turned and said, "You say you've bought it?" I assured her that I had, and she said yet again, "Nay, it is a little 'un". So I began to wonder if I would have any beast left at all by the time I got home!

But she became a grand animal and we were together for fourteen years, quite a bit longer than average. She produced some splendid calves, including Rosa, who was to replace Her Ladyship not only in my affections but went on to follow her mother by playing a significant role in a subsequent television programme.

Princes of Wales and Other Royals

In a roundabout way, I have had brief relationships with the last two Princes of Wales. When I was a little girl we had a royal blue tea tin bearing the likeness of Edward the Eighth, who abdicated to become the Duke of Windsor. I used to gaze at this tin and wonder at the grandeur of his titles, written in gold: King Beyond The Seas, Defender Of The Faith, Emperor Of India . . .

I was a schoolgirl when he gave up the throne and I recall feeling very sorry. I have nothing against his younger brother who unexpectedly became George the Sixth — a really good man in everyone's opinion — but I believe Edward would have made a fine monarch, too. It was such a pity that he met and became besotted with Mrs Wallis Simpson, who people said may have been something of an adventuress. I was too young to realise. I know he said that he couldn't carry on without the woman he loved, but it's clear, to me at least, from the photographs of the Duke down the years that he did not appear to be altogether a happy man.

I actually came face to face with the next — and present Prince of Wales. We met at the Royal Agricultural

Show a few years ago, and we had a long chat — such a thrill for me, because I have always liked him. So had a relative of mine by marriage, Lizzie Bayles, sadly no longer with us, who was to feature in the conversation. Prince Charles was obviously very well briefed about my background because he asked me how I was enjoying the benefit of running water in my cottage in Cotherstone (Low Birk Hatt farm had no taps) and talked about the Teesdale area. I knew he was familiar with our moors because he sometimes came for the grouse season. When Lizzie heard I was to meet the Prince of Wales, she was quite as excited as me and made me promise to give him her love. She had been a devoted admirer ever since he was born and had seen him at close quarters during one of his visits to Teesdale. So I mentioned this promise when the chance arose during our meeting, and he responded with such charm saying I must pass on his love to her!

I was told that the Princess of Wales knew about me, too (this always surprises me, but I suppose all those television programmes and books must be responsible). Sir Jimmy Savile, who apparently knew her quite well, mentioned this fact to me when we were at a party on the QE2. I saw her just once, at another party attended by many celebrities (Jimmy was one of them, but please don't place me in that bracket), held to celebrate the 150th anniversary of Thomas Cook, the travel company which had sponsored my "Innocent Abroad" television series. She was the guest of honour and appeared just as dinner was served and sat at the next table to me. But she seemed as shy and retiring as her husband was confident and outgoing — at least on that occasion. Barry Cockcroft, who was my escort, said she rarely lifted her head to look around during the meal. I am not aware that she spoke to anyone apart from those at her table and after one dance with, I believe, the chairman of Thomas Cook, she disappeared. Please do not conclude that I am being critical. That is just an honest reflection of that evening from where I was sitting. I don't blame her in the least because we now know just what pressure and unhappiness she was probably enduring around that time.

She was so pretty, and lively in the right circumstances, and worked so hard for good causes. But her marriage to Prince Charles turned out to be, in a different way, as unhappy an incident in Royal history as that of Mrs Simpson and the Duke of Windsor. And ended in real tragedy in that awful car crash.

I suppose most people remember where they were and what they were doing when they heard that dire news. I was in Llandudno, having just done "An Evening With", at a big hotel with Barry. It was a dismal journey back home.

I believe Charles and Diana to be admirable people who just weren't suited to each other. That may sound an obvious point to make after all we know now, but I was uneasy about the marriage from the outset. I was not prejudiced against either. It was just instinct. I even voiced my concern in the draft for one of my books, but that was during the time when everyone believed it to be a match as romantic as something out of a fairy tale so it was deemed unwise to print it.

It has been suggested that there may have been an element of an arrangement in that match, but, there again, it seems clear that the Prince of Wales' brother and sister had a free choice, and their unions didn't last either. I have been in the company of both Prince Andrew and Princess Anne, but did not have the opportunity to speak to either. I am not one to push myself forward on those occasions. But I really liked the look of Prince Andrew. I came near to him at a Royal Garden Party in the grounds of Buckingham Palace. I thought he was such a handsome man. I've never seen his former wife, Sarah Ferguson, in the flesh but she doesn't pretend to be anything other than what she is. What you see is what you get!

I think the Queen has done a difficult task really well. But I am all in favour of the Royal Family moving with the times. Some people want them to ride by in a gilded coach, and nothing more. I agree with those who wish to see a more friendly, approachable and down to earth attitude. The Royals in less formal places like Holland apparently ride bikes, and I don't see anything wrong in that. They are only flesh and blood with human frailties, like everyone else.

All things considered, I am in favour of a monarchy for this country. There are many examples of those without one which have not fared too well, at all. I think an hereditary monarch is far preferable to some power-mad upstart scheming and plotting to become president.

There has been some debate in newspapers about Britain becoming a republic, and speculation about who should become Head of State. The name of Mrs Thatcher was mentioned, and I believe that prospect was held to be the best argument for keeping the monarchy.

Do not ask me for my opinion on that particular issue. I am just a simple Daleswoman, not qualified to comment on political matters.

King George . . .
Standing At The
Gate of the Year

Another abiding memory of royalty for me happened at the very beginning of the last war when King George the Sixth spoke to the nation on the radio. The year was 1939 and it was his Christmas Day speech. Now I know he had a stammer to overcome but I thought he had a really fine speaking voice, very slow and clear.

I was only thirteen at the time, but I can still hear him reading some very moving words:

And I said to the man who stood at the gate of the year: "Give me a light that I may tread safely into the unknown". And he replied: "Go out into the darkness and put your hand into the hand of God. That shall be to you better than light and safer than a known way."

(M. Louise Haskins 1897-1957)

When poppy time comes round to remember those who gave their lives for us, there will be people saying "Oh, it's all those years ago, don't you think it's time to forget?" I say they should never be forgotten. What we enjoy now we owe to so many people, in uniform and out, the known and the unknown, our own countrymen and women and people from abroad. If ever I get to Hyde Park Corner, that's the message I'll put across!

The Unacceptable Face of the Media

You can see it on television, you read it in the newspapers . . . there seems to be this continual raking up of facts about people's private lives. Now evil and wrong-doing should be exposed, because that is in the best interests of the public. But I believe the media are now taking things too far, and people are being obliged to reveal matters about themselves which is really their own business. It is not necessary for anyone else to know because it does not harm or affect them, nor interfere with any public duties the person being pressurised may perform.

I am thinking particularly of a Minister of Agriculture, who has enough to worry about trying to solve the very serious problems of the farming community of this country without being hounded about something which shouldn't concern anyone else.

It has become too frequent, almost a craze. Good people as well as bad are having their lives torn apart. The media should be very careful before rushing to judgement. Some of their actions are totally unacceptable.

I went to the cinema occasionally in Barnard Castle. The films I particularly remember are *The Great Waltz* with the music of Johan Strauss, and *The Great Caruso*. Then once I went to stay with relatives in Piercebridge and saw *Maytime*.

Politics . . . and Religion

Politics and religion are two subjects which are usually discouraged when people gather to discuss the ways of the world, since they often lead to rancour. So I will tread carefully around this particular area.

For obvious reasons, I didn't have many chances to use my vote until I retired to Cotherstone. But I did get to the polling booth during the election that brought Tony Blair to power, and I don't mind revealing that I voted for the Labour candidate in my constituency, Mr Derek Foster, because I consider him to be both a good MP and a good man.

I suppose I tend to favour people who are obviously decent — I liked John Major, for instance, and my favourite American President of recent times was Jimmy Carter. To be fair to President Clinton, it's a shame that his private life is rather spoiling things. Maybe he isn't a bad President. But if you are the roving kind it is perhaps wiser to remain single, then there wouldn't be a wife and family involved. When Mr Clinton first stood for office, he had one trump card — he looked like President John F. Kennedy. But it seems he was similar in other ways . . . a case of history repeating itself.

As far as the New Labour people are concerned, I will have to reserve judgement simply because I am not properly acquainted with enough information to reach one. I rarely watch television at home because there are too many things in the way, don't have much time to listen to the radio (except for certain music programmes) and my eyes aren't up to reading newspapers much because the print is so small. However, Tony Blair seems to be a pleasant and well-meaning man trying to do a very tough job, and Mo Mowlem has clearly worked wonders in Northern Ireland. Since I know and like so many people over there I hope and pray she can persuade them to keep things stable.

Going back to the past, there is Winston Churchill, of course. Maybe he wasn't perfect and perhaps he made some blunders during the First World War. But I can say in all reverence: Thank God for him, because he was the right man at the right time for the Second.

Which thought leads me to the other perilous subject — religion. I lost the opportunity to attend chapel when our little one in Baldersdale closed down, so it was nice to be able to start again when I moved to Cotherstone. I go when I can.

But it is clear to me that there is a marked distinction between religion and Christianity. Sometimes they are not even on nodding acquaintance, because there is so much intolerance in the world. Northern Ireland is a classic example, and other faiths have similar problems. Although it is sad that churches and chapels have to close down through dwindling support, I think that there are people who don't worship regularly in public but still qualify as good Christians. That may be stating the obvious, but surely you should be judged by how you behave and treat people.

Religion can be a confusing business, even in small matters. In the Methodist faith, we have different branches. Recently, I asked one of my favourite preachers to explain the difference between Wesleyan Methodists and Primitive Methodists but didn't really understand.

My Uncle Tommy was a preacher, and generally good at public speaking. He was very well read and could quote passages from the Good Book from memory. He also had a fine sense of humour. When he was asked, as he sometimes was, to stand up and give a vote of thanks or the like, you never knew what he was going to say next.

I was always pleased when he sat down!

One summer many years ago we had such a long and dry spell. It gave us one of the very few really good haytimes we ever had and the water in the reservoir by Low Birk Hatt was very low. One evening I went down there with a black dog we had called Peter, gathering sticks for kindling and enjoying the beauty and tranquility. I stayed so long that Peter went back home without me, which understandably caused concern. But I just lost all track of time. Water is so therapeutic, whether it be a singing stream, a reservoir lit by a sunset, or the mighty ocean.

Mason's Dog Oil . . . and other Country Remedies

When you lived in a remote place like Baldersdale, particularly in days gone by, people often had their own way of dealing with aches, pains and other minor ailments. It wasn't always easy to get to a doctor, or afford the latest medication from the pharmacy. My mother used wintergreen and knitbone, which have been country remedies for generations, and was never without aconite, an absolute essential for colds. We also used to put it in the water for the animals.

I believe there are things provided by Nature which could be beneficial if we only knew more about them. Gypsies are supposed to have a knowledge of plants and herbs that can help to heal. But there would have to be more research or the unwise could end up poisoning themselves. That thought reminds me of an occasion long ago when a calf down the dale became poorly. The couple who owned it were telling my Uncle Tommy, who came to look after Low Birk Hatt when my father died at an early age, what they had given this calf. Uncle was very good with animals, might have been a veterinary given different circumstances, and was often called in to help when animals in the dale were ill. They said they had tried half a dozen remedies, and the wife commented that if the calf did survive they wouldn't know what had cured it. And if it died, what had killed it?

Recently, I came across a rather unusual remedy, made by the same family in Lancashire for more than seventy years, according to the label.

Mason's Dog Oil.

As the name suggests, I assume it was originally intended to use on dogs. But a friend of mine told me the story of a man who had a racing dog, a greyhound I believe, which he treated with Mason's Dog Oil. He had a problem with his hands and realised that after rubbing the oil into his dog they felt a lot better. I was sufficiently impressed to acquire some for myself. It is no cure, but it can soothe some painful conditions. It comes in a yellow plastic container with a black lid, and the label says it's a blend of natural mineral and vegetable oils, listed as rapeseed oil and petroleum jelly, contains no animal products and no perfumes. And it is only for external use. It also says that should symptoms persist you should consult a physician, so it must be for humans as well as dogs.

I know it really works. One winter day, a little old lady slipped in icy conditions on the pavement near my cottage and injured her shoulder. She had been to the doctor for something to relieve the pain, but you know how slow things are to heal when you are getting on in years. So I took her a pot of Mason's Dog Oil. She was rather sceptical at the time, but when I saw her later and made some reference to it, she exclaimed: "Oh, I put it on every night, I've used it nearly all!"

Forty Years On . . .
The Dentist and Me

I do see a doctor on a fairly regular basis these days, but it's a very different story with my dental health. It must be forty years since I last visited a dentist. And I don't propose to go again, unless forced to!

My top set of teeth are all false. They began to come out when I was a youngster and Grandma Hauxwell took me to a dentist who chose not to use much anaesthetic. It was a traumatic experience.

When it was deemed necessary to remove all the rest of my top set, another dentist was located in Barnard Castle who was more liberal in the prevention of pain. That was in 1947 when the worst winter I can recall closed down Baldersdale. I had to wait for the thaw before we could get out into the outside world. A kind neighbour accompanied me on that occasion.

I am still using the same set he made for me. They are a bit worn now but still serviceable. The lower teeth are all my own — those that survive, that is. The last one to be removed happened on that occasion forty years or so ago.

I now possess five reasonable lower teeth, though they are starting to part a bit, and two funny stumps — one on either side of the others.

So I hope for two things . . . that they don't start to ache, and I don't break my false set!

I am very attached to The Great One, my central heating boiler, but I have never understood its workings, how to switch it on and off, and never will. Sometimes it's on when it shouldn't be, which is an extravagance. I rely on the goodness of neighbours to attend to it. The grand little lady who sold me the house told me that the milkman was very obliging and understood how to regulate the Great One. He has retired now to a little bungalow just out of the village, but still pops in occasionally to sort it out when there is no-one else available.

Poets, Pit Ponies and the Teesdale Pimpernel

Poetry, like music, has always been a source of comfort and pleasure for me and sometimes I am able to indulge in both verse and song when I attend the concerts given by my long-time favourites, the Cockfield Methodist Male Voice Choir. In between the numbers, they allow me to recite a few lines, usually from the poets of Teesdale — and we have a goodly number for our size and population.

I have become associated with one particular poet, Richard Watson, who worked down the local lead mines and is often referred to as "The Bard of Teesdale". That is because I often conclude my "Evenings With" by reading a poem of his entitled "The Teesdale Hills", which aptly conveys my own love of my homeland. Another local man with a fine talent was William Langstaff, who also wrote lines which remind me particularly of Low Birk Hatt and the surrounding countryside:

> Lone, silent hills,
> Clear, singing streams.
> Among them, we're close to God.

70

There is yet another Teesdale poet who can stir my imagination, and I find myself inclining more to his work when I do my public readings. Walter Dent Bayles was born in 1903 at Stainmoor, where my parents originated, and part of his working life was spent down mines, like Richard Watson. And he, too, was a lover of Teesdale but did not live to see his work in print. A limited edition was published in 1996, nine years after he was buried at Middleton-in-Teesdale. It's possible he was akin to me since one of my middle names is Bayles, like my father. Walter was friendly with my late cousin, Norman Bayles, and his wife (mentioned previously), Lizzie, and I remember him when I was a schoolgirl coming with a group to sing and recite at our chapel in Baldersdale. He had a fine singing voice.

I particularly like one of his poems which he wrote in response to one entitled "Owd Ponies", written by a lady about pit ponies from the miner's point of view. Those poor little creatures were obviously still toiling down mines at the time because in a preface Walter wrote: "I regret that there are several mines in County Durham where ponies are still used for haulage. I worked for a number of years in mines where ponies were used, and would like to pass on to you a poem I have composed from the pony's point of view, to all who are detailed to handle them."

He entitled it "A Pit Pony's Prayer in Verse", and here are some lines from it:

> Be kind to me, oh master,
> I have my feelings, too.

But I respond to treatment,
Just like you humans do.

When you give me your orders,
Help me to understand.
Be sure my limbs become not sore,
From chain or harness band.

And, master, when you're angry
With conditions black as night.
Remember, though not human,
I, too, love the sun and light.

So now, as I'm entrusted,
Daily to your care.
I hope that He who made us both,
Will hear a pony's prayer.

Walter also wrote another poem to celebrate an exclusive botanical feature of Teesdale. There is a type of blue gentian which, apparently, grows only in Teesdale and Switzerland. It blooms in parts of Upper Teesdale and though I have never seen one myself friends of mine have and I possess a photograph. There was a controversy some years ago when they built Cow Green reservoir above High Force, the famous waterfall in Teesdale, because it was said to disturb the gentian's natural habitat.

This rare flower inspired Walter to write "To the Blue Gentian", which includes the lines:

Thy yearly visitations to
   Teesdale's windswept hills.
Doth mystify the gardener's hand,
   no matter how he tills.
The botanists have taken thee,
   applying various skills.
In sad despair, they hear thee cry
   "Oh, take me to my hills!"
Though we may tramp the universe,
   or sail the seas around.
In Switzerland and Teesdale,
   alone thou wilt be found.

A more contemporary poet is my friend, Jack Robinson, a proud Yorkshireman who has publicly opposed that part of the White Rose county where I was born and raised being placed in County Durham in 1974. He celebrated Yorkshire Day each August 1st in the Rose and Crown at Mickleton, which he ran until his retirement. It bore a defiant sign outside proclaiming "Welcome to Yorkshire"! I must say I agree with Jack, and will always regard myself as a Yorkshirewoman.

Jack is a distant relative of mine — a quarter cousin, I believe — and it happens that August 1st is my birthday so he invited me to attend every celebration since he launched it in 1984. He writes poems about me, adding a new verse every year as a birthday present to one entitled "The Fields of Low Birk Hatt". He wrote one as recently as 1996, called "The Teesdale Pimpernel". That's me, it seems!

This is an extract:

Have you heard of Hannah Hauxwell,
    the Teesdale Pimpernel?
She's always gadding off these days,
    her life story to tell.
A total change from Birk Hatt,
    when in the winter's cold,
She broke the ice on frozen stream,
    to water cattle in the fold.
She used same source for water,
    to make a cup of tea.
No running water there on tap,
    unlike you and me.
The winter's day were long,
    short was the light of day.
Through snowdrifts she would struggle,
    to take her cattle hay.
Alec Donaldson from the Yorkshire Post,
    he was the first to write,
About this lady of the hills,
    her lifestyle and her plight.
Yorkshire Television followed,
    with the making of a film.
Produced by Barry Cockcroft,
    she thinks the world of him.
To foreign parts he's taken her,
    that once were just a dream.
Electric trains on railways,
    they've done away with steam.
She travelled on an ocean liner,
    to the United States of A.

Trip up the Eiffel Tower,
  not for me she'd say.
People come to see her,
  and to wish her well.
It's sometimes hard to find her,
  The Teesdale Pimpernel!

The Two Reginalds . . .And My Musical Obsession

Much as I love poetry, music is most certainly closest to my heart. My attachment began as a child, listening to my mother play. She was a fine musician, far better than I will ever be. I did take piano lessons for three months or so, but the lady who taught me got married and it had to stop. To be truthful, I wasn't coming on so well, anyway. And for good or ill, I found I could play better by ear, which is a lot easier than thrashing it out from sheet music. I can read music a little, but only slowly and with difficulty, the right hand being better than the left.

The organ is my favourite instrument, and Mother brought one with her when she married Daddy. I still have it, although it is no longer serviceable. I actually have another two, including Mr Hammond (also disabled at the moment), so you could say I am organ daft! The only time I listen regularly to the radio during the week is on a Tuesday evening, when Nigel Ogden presents a programme of organ music recordings. I do tune in on Sundays, too, until it's time to go to chapel.

I had a wonderful experience recently when I was on a week's tour of Lincolnshire presenting "Evenings With Hannah Hauxwell" in local libraries. One day my hosts took me to see an old cinema, called The Kinema, unusually situated in a wood in Woodhall Spa, and that had a magnificent old organ. When I arrived it was being played by the gentleman who I assume owned The Kinema, and when he discovered I was fascinated by organs he asked me to try it out. But the real thrill came when it turned out to be one of those that rise from below, like the one at the Tower Ballroom in Blackpool. You went behind and below the organ, then rose up whilst playing just like Reginald Dixon. The instrument itself was also remarkable, a Compton with at least two manuals, red in colour and decorated with Geisha girls. I played a gospel piece I know by heart, called "He Touched Me".

Of course, there were two famous Reginalds associated with the organ — Mr Dixon in Blackpool and Mr Forte of the BBC — and I was privileged to see and hear both of them play. It was on a chapel trip to Blackpool that I went to see Mr Blackpool as they called him (I had listened to him on the radio as well, of course). His upwardly mobile organ was cream in colour and he wore a suit to match and started with his signature tune, "I Do Like To Be Beside The Seaside".

Mr Forte actually came to play twice in Teesdale, a real treat for all his admirers in the area. Mother and I went to both, first to the Bourne Methodist Chapel in Middleton-in-Teesdale, a really fine building which is sadly closed now. We went to stay overnight with my cousin, Norman Bayles, and his wife, Lizzie, at their small farm just outside Mickleton and it turned out to be a memorable night. The chapel had a fine organ, so good that Mr Forte remarked on its quality. We sat in the gallery and he was just as personable as he was on the radio, starting with his signature tune to "let us know who he was"! I particularly remember his version of "Poet and Peasant", which mother used to play. We had a soloist, a local man called Mr Arnold Grieve, who sang "Oh, Ruddier Than The Cherry" and "Pale Hands I Love". A wonderful partnership of organ and voice. Mr Grieve received praise from the great man, too. As it happens, he lives just along the village from me and, remarkably, is still singing to appreciative audiences.

At the end of the recital, I had the thrill of coming face to face with Mr Forte to obtain a signature on his photograph, which I still have somewhere. They were being sold for two shillings and sixpence, a tidy sum in those days but equivalent to twelve and a half pence these days. That is the only time I have ever asked for anyone's autograph (conversely, I must have been asked myself many a hundred times in recent years).

Mr Forte came later to Trinity Chapel in Barnard Castle and Mother and I travelled to see him again. Although he was just as good, it wasn't as happy an experience as the first occasion because it was essential we caught the last bus back to Cotherstone which meant we were on edge during the later stages keeping an eye on the clock. We were obliged to leave before the finish.

Oddly, there were even more Reginalds playing the organ to public acclaim in those days. I remember one radio programme which featured four of them, Messrs Forte and Dixon and two not quite so famous called Reginald New and Reginald Porter-Brown.

I believe Reginald Forte eventually went for a long time to play in the United States, and even took his organ with him which must have caused some transportation problems. In my opinion, he was the best of the BBC Theatre organists which, incidentally, included another celebrity who came to Teesdale — Sandy McPherson. He became well-known during the war, playing requests on the radio for the forces. Mother went to his recital, but for some reason I didn't accompany her. But we both went to hear another BBC organist, a lady called Ena Baga, when she played locally.

So you see, many of my musical memories revolve around the organ. It's a bit of an obsession, I suppose. If I was to be reincarnated, I would choose to return to earth as a combination of Reginald Dixon and Reginald Forte!

In the meantime I shall carry on playing for my own pleasure without inflicting my efforts on other ears too often. It is a dream of mine to own a really good organ like a Wurlitzer or a Compton. Not a huge thing . . . there are smaller versions available. I don't require more than two manuals but I would want as many stops as possible. They don't make the old stops now, the ones you pulled out and pushed in, but I prefer levers rather than buttons. My repertoire tends to vary but consists basically of gospel numbers and romantic tunes like "Smile Awhile" and "Softly Awakes My Heart". I have tried to play "The Lost Chord" but I couldn't find it!

The most impressive instrument I have ever encountered is situated in Durham Cathedral. I was a guest at a function at Durham Castle a couple of years ago and after dinner we were all taken to the cathedral to hear a short recital by the resident organist. The sound was amazing, like thunder at times, but his choice of music suited me. He even played one of my favourites, "Moonlight and Roses". I am not enamoured of some of the dry old highbrow composers, such as Bach.

Then I was taken to see the organ close to, which meant climbing some narrow, twisty steps. The controls reminded me of the bridge of the QE2. There could have been five or more manuals, with numerous keys and buttons all over the place.

This time I wasn't offered the chance to play, although I have been kindly allowed to try some splendid organs.

Bad Seams, Dutch Trousers and Exclusive Headgear

Now I do like nice clothes, but I suppose high fashion and me are usually strangers. I like to wear comfortable old things, especially when I am working about the house and doing errands in the village. I much prefer trousers to skirts, and am particularly attached to one pair which took a deal of time and effort — and some pain — to resurrect. But it was a necessary labour because as in the case of shoes previously mentioned, trouser manufacturers don't seem to realise that we all come in different sizes and shapes. At least, they don't seem to cater for my size and shape!

These particular trousers, which have been described as Dutch in style because they billow out like those worn by people in old Dutch paintings, started out in life at Low Birk Hatt maybe thirty years ago as a pair of corduroys, a fabric I like very much. They had belonged to someone else in the household, and I fished them out because I hadn't anything else suitable at the time. When the time came to patch both knees and I needed cloth, my friend Richard at the Youth Hostel in Baldersdale gave me a pair of his old jeans — nicely washed, of course — and my old cords were revived. But during one recent summer the left leg began to go home, as we say, so I bent to the task again. I applied more denim patches over the original patches, by dint of some intricate stitching, and worked on a lining which didn't quite match the size of the rest of the material and may account for the Dutch effect.

It was a tough job. I worked for two whole weeks before I got it right, and could have cried many a time. But it was worth it because they are so comfortable.

Sewing is where my time, labour and eyesight go. It's a perpetual problem because so many clothes these days seem — as my mother and Grandma Hauxwell used to say — to be blown together. I come from a family of seamstresses for Grandma was an accomplished sewer, producing lovely quilts, and Mother was a trained dressmaker. So I do know shoddy work when I see it. Take seams, for instance. At the time of writing, I am working on a tweed coat which has seams less than half an inch. Now tweed is a fairly loosely woven material, so I have to overstitch all the seams which, to use a modern expression, is labour intensive.

Although I wear old things on a day to day basis (and they are becoming thin and weary despite spasms of attention), the clothes I go away in for public appearances must be in good order. I am nearly always rushing to avoid being very late, and I can't be doing with finding at the last minute that a hole has developed or a button missing. So I go over every article of clothing to ensure they are always ready for the road. It's a weakness of mine.

I sometimes think that clothes should be turned inside out when they are to sell, so that people can see what they are really like. It appears to be all economy these days, cutting down on material and producing them on a conveyor belt system. It does annoy me. I seem to spend half my life making good the defects, and all by hand. I do have more than one sewing machine, and intend to get them going one day. There is a good old Singer treadle machine which came from home, but the pedal is stuck and it's away from good light. A kind neighbour has offered to mend it. As for the others, I either can't get at them or I don't understand how they work.

I have to do all my washing be hand, too. There are washing machines in the house, but it's the same story. There's a little one in the kitchen and an automatic ready plumbed in housed in a cupboard in the passage. I cannot use either at the moment because they are buried under all the boxes containing the belongings I brought down from the farm.

My favourite attire at all times is a pair of trousers and a good, roomy jumper. If I can get away with them even on formal occasions, then I will. I hasten to add that I wouldn't display the Dutch trousers outside the village! I don't get dressed up to go to the chapel, but cover up with a good coat. They haven't turned me away yet! Anyway, does the Good Lord mind whether one is dressed to the nines? I think there are those who attach too much importance to dress, and not enough to what people are. Some would welcome Old Nick himself if he appeared beautifully dressed!

On the subject of high fashion, I can claim to possess headwear which is both specially designed and totally exclusive to me. But don't take me seriously. It was inspired by a sudden change in the weather and I mislaid one of the two headscarves I normally wear. The sole survivor wasn't warm enough. So I found a rollneck jumper which was too small for me, pulled the bottom up through the neck and with some strong string — ravellings from sacks, which isn't easy to get now — drew it up together using the arms to tie it. It worked well, so I was encouraged to make another, more superior version which I wear when the occasion demands something a little better!

Make Do and Mend . . . and the Inside Out Coat That Went With Uffa

Make Do and Mend . . . that was one of the clarion calls of the last war, along with Dig for Victory and Even the Walls Have Ears!

The Dutch trousers and exclusive headwear constitute a fair example of making the most of everything, and you certainly didn't have to tell the elder members of the Hauxwell family to make do and mend. They had been practising it since the dark days of the Depression in the Thirties, and probably even before that. I can tell you a tale about one garment which passed down the generations and finished up comforting a wonderful companion of mine: a dog called Uffa.

It was a trap coat made from a good thick tweed material — in fact, I've never seen cloth to match it since. Uncle was given it by friends during the War and he passed it on to me. When it became a bit worn on the outside and the herringbone showed through, it was unpicked and mother turned it inside out. How she managed I don't know because it was going on for a quarter of an inch thick, with double seams. The inside was a lovely grey-green colour, so it had another life on my back. Thirty years or so later it came to the end of its useful life and I gave it to Uffa to sleep on.

We had several dogs at Low Birk Hatt — Roy and Peter are well remembered — but Uffa was rather special to me. He was a border collie and came as a puppy from friends in Halifax after the first television programme, "Too Long A Winter", transmitted in January, 1973. He had such beautiful eyes, and was the first dog I had owned for a good while. I don't think he was ever very strong and in the early days I fed him on the sort of dog food everyone in the dale used, a kind of split maize or Indian corn which looked like cornflakes. You added boiling water to it. He began to take poorly, so I called the veterinary who said he was lacking vitamins. He gave Uffa an injection and the effect bordered on the miraculous. Within an hour he was another dog. I was also advised to change his diet, to Winalot and a little Marmite. Further injections were necessary but then he began to have fits. The vet prescribed some tablets but the time arrived when I knew it had become more serious. Whenever I came into the house he always used to meet me at the door leading from the kitchen to the front room. But one day, he wasn't there . . .

I sent for the vet again and though he was very busy he came that night at ten o'clock. He was a nice man, very good with dogs and knelt down on the floor to examine poor Uffa. There was another injection and more tablets, but he told me that he was a very sick dog and we would have to see what developed. A younger vet came to examine Uffa the following day, and said I should think about having him put to sleep. I asked him to wait a day or two, but, it proved inevitable. There comes a time when it's the only thing and the kindest thing to do.

It upset me so much. I was desolate without Uffa.

He lived in the house and slept in a leather chair with that old coat for warmth. I wrapped him up in it and buried him in the pasture, a little way from the house.

Tim . . . and the Prospect of A Stray at the Door

Tim was my last dog. He was a lively little Jack Russell terrier, who was alright on his own but not with other dogs. Tim would have fought a lion if he had encountered one.

More difficulties arose when I had to go away so much, two six week tours in Europe and the United States, for instance. Friends in the village were kind enough to look after him in the early days, but then it became necessary to arrange long-term boarding for him. They were very good to him at the kennels.

Sadly, Tim died, too.

Although I love dogs very much, I cannot have one in my present situation because I am still frequently away from home. I just hope that no pathetic and appealing little stray doesn't land on my doorstep one day.

I would be sorely tempted . . .

Ireland — Cross Border Experiences . . . and a Midnight Mystery

I have developed a great liking for the people of Ireland. I think they are friendly, warm-hearted and genuine — and that includes both sides of that troubled island. I know, because I have travelled across the divide from Ulster to Eire and spent several weeks there in the last seven years. My association with Ireland began in 1992, when I was invited to appear on the Gerry Kelly television show, which goes out from Belfast every Friday night. This came about because my programmes and books had been well received across the entire country.

Altogether, I have been across the water half a dozen times or more — by boat, at first. A very pleasant gentleman called Paul Madeley, who organised guests for Gerry Kelly from the mainland, did suggest that I fly to Belfast but when I pointed out that I was not too happy with that arrangement did kindly organise a sea crossing. It seems that I was only the second out of hundreds of guests down the years to make such a request. But I do not like flying, and probably never will.

They must have been keen to have me because it was a long and expensive business, although I didn't realise it at the time. My good friend, Kelvin Walker, who is our village taxi driver, had to convey me all the way to Stranraer in Scotland to catch the ferry to Belfast. It was a long drive, and he had to come all the way to Stranraer again to pick me up when I returned.

Gerry Kelly turned out to be a lovely man, a pleasure to meet, and the interview seemed to go down really well. Indeed, I was subsequently invited to make a repeat visit to appear again with Gerry. That first appearance seemed to open the door for me in Ireland because I have been a regular visitor ever since, the last occasion being in September, 1998. My second trip was at the invitation of the Belfast Central Mission, a Methodist organisation which does a lot of good in the city under difficult circumstances. Their buildings had suffered damage in the conflict. I have been their guest now on four occasions, raising money by doing my "Evenings With". A gentleman called Paul Clark, a programme presenter in Belfast himself, conducted the interviews.

This, in turn, led to an invitation to help a Presbyterian community in Armagh, which I believe is a particularly troubled place. Their church was left in a really bad state after a bomb attack so I offered to try and raise funds for the re-building. And this time I made an exception about the travel arrangements because of the expense and agreed to fly. I had, in fact, flown previously when I returned from the United States after completing the "Hannah USA" television series — all the way from

Dallas to Gatwick, so I wasn't a novice. I went in a small plane from Teesside airport and arrived to a wonderful welcome. They even organised a reception at the town hall and presented me with a plaque. I stayed with Ian and Lily Adair, who had visited me in Cotherstone to issue an invitation. Ian was an RUC officer of some distinction, a good man who worked for both sides of the community. Paul Clark came to interview me in a large school hall but it still wasn't big enough for all those who wanted to buy tickets. That is why I came back for a repeat appearance in September of 1998 — by plane, this time from Leeds-Bradford airport. Thankfully, the hall was pretty full once more, and afterwards I was rather thrilled to be taken by Mr Adair to see and admire the restored church. I was allowed to play the organ — not for an audience, but purely for my own pleasure.

It was from Armagh on my first visit that I crossed the border to Eire, at the invitation of another gentleman who called on me at my cottage (I do get a lot of surprise visitors, sometimes from places as far afield as Canada, and even New Zealand). Roger O'Farrell lives in County Cork, and drove to Armagh to fetch me. I did yet another "Evening With" in a school hall. Indeed, I enjoyed the hospitality of the local community not once but twice, for I was pressed again to return later on. And I ended up on television again when a young man called Pat Walsh tracked me down after trying to find me in England at first. He arranged for me to return to Dublin at a later date to appear on the Pat Kenny Show. Another happy experience. I have to say that I found the people of the South of Ireland to be just as good, friendly and homely as in the North. I must have met both Protestants and Catholics in large numbers but I never could tell you the difference between them.

I must confess that I didn't see much physical evidence of the bitterness which has torn apart Ulster for so long. On my visits to the Belfast Mission I stayed in a private house on the outskirts of the city so I was not confronted with the graffiti on the walls and gable ends of houses, or much evidence of the road blocks which used to be so common. I did see a group of young soldiers once, plus a military vehicle, and some men with dark, padded jackets which I took to be policemen.

One evening I went to do an "Evening" in a chapel a long drive from Armagh in Five Mile Town, so called because it was five miles from anywhere else. I was greeted by members of the local council, who presented me with a lovely glass paperweight as a memento. On the way back there was very little traffic on the road and, although I wasn't frightened, it did cross my mind that, well, this was Northern Ireland and it could be anyone coming towards you, and not necessarily a friend.

But there was one strange and worrying experience when I returned to Belfast for my second appearance on the Gerry Kelly Show. This time, along with the rest of the guests, I was booked into a different hotel. Apparently it is wise to ring the changes like that in Belfast for security reasons. The show lasts for an hour and a half so we were late arriving back at the hotel. We were all relaxing and chatting — the other guests were very interesting and included the actress Paula Wilcox, with whom I had a long conversation, and Samantha Fox, the well-known model, when I was informed that someone was on the telephone for me. I thought it curious, since it had gone midnight, and so was Paul Madeley, the man who organised the guests, when I told him about the call. He said it was not public knowledge that we were staying at this hotel. The man had said he wanted me to appear on another show — I'm not sure whether it was radio or television, but it sounded very odd. Almost like a play. He said he was going to act the part of someone who wanted to meet me. I was not at all enthusiastic. Paul became even more concerned when he could not recognise the name the man had given me, although he was well acquainted with most of the media people in Belfast. So he started phoning round his contacts, one after another. It went on until three o'clock in the morning until Paul finally found someone who knew the man, who turned out to be genuine.

It was extraordinary how one innocent phone call could cause so much worry. I suppose it was a measure of the tension that cast such a long shadow over Northern Ireland.

I never did appear on the mystery man's show!

The Great Railway Adventure

Drama may be too strong a word for it, but I did become involved in an adventure following my appearance on the Pat Kenny television show in Dublin. The subsequent events certainly caused consternation in some quarters. For this particular trip I had been kindly allowed by Pat Walsh, the gentleman organising it, to travel by my preferred route — by sea. This time I travelled in Kelvin's taxi to Leeds, where I boarded a special bus taking people to Holyhead to catch the ferry. This route was chosen because I had two engagements to fulfil in Leeds after my date in Dublin, so a return on the bus back to Leeds from Holyhead was obviously the sensible arrangement.

Everything in Ireland progressed smoothly, and after the programme Pat took me to meet his family in Cobh, where the QE2 sometimes docks, before escorting me to Dun Laoghaire in good time to catch the boat back. He saw me safely in the queue to check in before saying farewell. Then the trouble started. There had been some problem with the boat we were supposed to travel on, and the company which ran it had arranged for its passengers to join another service. But as we waited to board, an announcement was made: the boat was full, they could take no more. So there I was — stranded, along with a number of others. It took until one o'clock in the morning to find hotels in Dun Laoghaire. There appeared to be only one man available to sort it all out. But I was very fortunate. I met two gentlemen in the middle of all this confusion who recognised me, and I don't know what I would have done without their help. They were Irish, on their way to Leeds like me and were to become, as things turned out, my long-term travelling companions.

We ended up in the same hotel, and had to be up and moving next day by 7a.m. to go to the harbour and start queueing again. And, would you believe, the same thing happened. The boat filled up and we had to wait for the next one, which meant that I missed the bus connection to Leeds. So, of course, did my new friends, Jim McCarthy and his brother-in-law, Joseph O'Rourke, who lived in Leeds and had been to a family reunion in Ireland.

By the time we landed in Holyhead, the alarm bells were ringing. When I didn't appear among the passengers on the bus on its arrival in Leeds, the people there to meet me (the organisers of the first event I was booked for) rang Kelvin back in Cotherstone. He, in turn, phoned Barry Cockcroft, who sprang into immediate action. Many telephone calls later he established that I was still in Holyhead, and even managed to persuade someone at the ferry terminal to find me and bring me to the telephone. So at least he confirmed that I was back in the country, which was a start! But when I told him that the only way to Leeds available then was by railway and that the journey required me to change trains, he began to worry all over again. He knew me well enough to realise that a complicated procedure like that was certain to end in disaster. So he obtained an assurance from British Rail — he even involved the railway police — that my progress would be monitored and the staff at Chester station, where apparently I was due to change, would find me and put me on the right connection. He then telephoned my hosts in Leeds to inform them of my new arrival time.

Unfortunately, I disappeared . . . swallowed up by the rail network. Along with my two friends. When I didn't show up in Leeds for the second time, Barry was alerted again. I believe he was not too pleased with British Rail (which still ran the railways then), and the poor people who had travelled to meet me again weren't very happy, either. And they kept on trying, all through the day and into the evening scrutinising the passengers alighting from every train I might possibly be on. Barry embarked on a telephone marathon, urging British Rail to use every resource to try and find me. And there I was, sitting on a train we had boarded in Holyhead wondering why it was going on and on such a long time. So did Jim and Joseph, because they, too, were under the impression that we had to change trains somewhere. But I don't recall it ever stopping. Anyway, we shared some sandwiches which Pat's mother, bless her, had made me for the journey. They were such gentlemen, really magnificent.

Eventually, we fetched up in London — at Euston station! Barry's persistence had obviously worked because there was a delegation of railway officials there to meet us, carry our luggage and even pay for a taxi to take us to King's Cross station to catch a train for Leeds. Jim very generously telephoned his wife to ask her to organise overnight accommodation for me. She was there to meet us when we arrived in Leeds, and so were the people who had expected me to turn up about twelve hours earlier. Jim's offer of hospitality was not required because they had made arrangements. It was very nearly midnight, and everyone was exhausted.

At least I made it in time for both appearances in Leeds. As the saying goes, better late than never!

A sense of humour is an important asset, and a one-time good neighbour of mine from long ago certainly possessed one. Vince Anderson farmed Clove Lodge and I well recall one day when we were chatting and I admired his black and white collie dog.

"Aye", he said, "but he wasn't fairly close when brains were handed out!"

More Railway Perils . . . and the Dreaded Escalators

There have been other occasions on railway journeys when I have encountered difficulties, but I have always been particularly fortunate when assistance was urgently required — as in the epic trip from Ireland to Yorkshire. I have to say that the age of chivalry is not yet dead.

Once, there was a very worrying incident when I travelled to Southampton to board the QE2. There was a bomb scare and the train was stopped at Birmingham New Street. We had to evacuate the train, with our luggage, and get out of the station. I was struggling along with my cases when I came face to face with an escalator. Now I dread those things. On one occasion in New York whilst filming "Hannah USA" I was supposed to go to the top of Trump Tower, a very extravagant building on Fifth Avenue. There was only one way up, via an escalator. It was an extremely long and horrid kind, and I just could not make it — although I did try. Barry Cockcroft was obliged to cancel the planned sequence.

Anyway, as we hurried away from the alleged danger (it must have been a malicious hoax), there it was. I would much rather climb any height by steps, but this was supposed to be an emergency. However, help was at hand. A young gentleman must have noticed my discomfort and stepped in, although he had a wife and young family plus luggage to worry about as well. He still found the time to assist me to safety — I do not think I could have managed it on my own. He was also on hand to assist me back down when, after a delay, we were told we could return to the train and continue the journey.

I have a policy which never varies when I travel on the railways. Somebody has to put me on the train at one end like a big parcel, or I would likely board the wrong one. At the other end I stay put on the platform where I get off and don't move unless and until someone comes to claim me. I also have a plan of action if no-one turns up at all. I would proceed to the lost property office!

Once I did arrive in London to find the platform empty of welcoming faces. So I remained on the spot as everyone left. I must have looked a trifle forlorn because — yet again — a gentleman came to help, asking me if I was alright and was I being met. I suppose he may have recognised me, but he was so polite that I'm sure he would have been concerned whoever I was. All was well in the end — the people due to meet me had been delayed.

There have been several similar acts of kindness on my rail travels, such as willing hands to assist with luggage. And to be fair to British Rail, there was one time when they went out of their way to overcome a problem. I was due to board the direct train from Darlington to Leeds, but was informed I would have to change at York. That would have been a nightmare for me. But a very pleasant porter — I had seen him before — escorted me on to the train, then telephoned to York and arranged for someone to meet me there and put me on the right train to Leeds.

I suppose I must be a human version of Paddington Bear. Perhaps I should travel with a notice hung round my neck: "Please look after this bear" (or maybe replace the word "bear" with "bumpkin"!)

I was asked if I wanted to learn to drive now that I am retired. I replied that I have come to the conclusion as I go around that there's plenty of fools on the road behind the wheel of a car without me joining them. I would be a menace to myself and everyone else!

His Majesty . . . and Other Close Friends

On the subject of Teddy bears, I was nearer seventy than sixty before I had one of my own. No-one every gave me a Teddy during my childhood, and I had to wait until I moved to Cotherstone before Teddies entered my life. Now, I don't know how many I have. Word got around that I liked Teddies and people keep presenting me with various specimens of the cuddly breed.

I love them all and they are all known simply as Teddy, except one. He is rather larger, was presented to me during a visit to Grange-over-Sands, one of my favourite places, and he has a title rather than a name: His Majesty. There is an even bigger one which has sat in my front window for some time. He had to wear a plastic mac because it sometimes rained in through a defective window frame, which I have recently had replaced. There's a story attached to Big Teddy. I was appearing at a chapel on the Fylde Coast to raise funds when a little girl won two Teddies in a competition. One was so large that she couldn't get her arms round it, and she offered it to me. I tried to say no, but she insisted. A lovely gesture from one so young. Another rather special one came from the United States.

Of all my collection, I have had to buy only one. I came across him in a charity shop in Barnard Castle, a little fellow sitting on the floor in the window looking very droopy and pathetic. Coming to pieces, actually. I gave a pound for him, took him home and mended him.

There is just one other of my furry friends who has a name, and he is a brown and white dog with floppy ears. I acquired him on a visit to Leake in Lincolnshire (kindly given by the lady I stayed with), and he is quite a character. I understand he cost forty-five pounds when new. I called him Boo, after a real dog belonging to some friends of mine.

They are all good company. I speak to them frequently, and they never argue with me. And I can tell them anything because they are so discreet. They live all over the house, including the bathroom and my bedroom, and when I look at them I am reminded of the people who gave them to me

They all came with love and kindness, and you cannot say better than that . . .

Hoarding . . . and the Five Year Plan(s)

I must confess to being a hoarder — world class, some say. It is very difficult for me to discard anything, however small and insignificant, so I am not at one with this throwaway society.

My home is rather full of possessions acquired over nearly threequarters of a century, so much so that there is very little space left to even sit down. The place is piled high with boxes and parcels which came down from Low Birk Hatt more than ten years ago and which I haven't yet had time or opportunity to unpack. I'm not sure what some of them contain, but they will all be valuable to me and I cannot part with them. Many hold precious memories from the past.

But it does make life difficult, and items such as the sewing machines and washing machines have been swallowed up. I did start with a Five Year Plan to sort everything out, but that has by necessity been doubled — and then some!

The post I receive is another problem. I used to get a lot and it still arrives in quantity, particularly at Christmas and my birthday. Some people also send books to sign and return, but I do not have the opportunity to deal with those, either. Others have formed the impression that I am lonely and have time weighing heavy on my hands. They write and offer to become regular pen-pals, which is very kind and thoughtful of them. Most of these end up with Barry Cockcroft, redirected from Yorkshire Television (with whom he is no longer connected), and he very politely declines on my behalf.

It's all I can do to cope with the essentials, such as gas and electricity bills. I don't like the direct debit idea, preferring to keep control of my financial affairs, and I find my local post office just across the road to be the best way to organise payments. They are most helpful. But I do get behind and make mistakes sometimes, and along come those letters and bills printed in red!

No, paperwork and me just don't go together!

Isolation . . . and the Man Who Would Not Speak

Being on my own in a remote place didn't scare me. I would sometimes walk back alone from a friend's house in the small hours of the morning, and never give a thought to the possibility that I might be vulnerable.

Only on two or three occasions throughout my long years of isolation did I feel some concern. One May evening when the light was just fading and I was still outside working around the byre, a man came through the iron gate and on to my land. I called out a greeting, as is my wont . . . and he didn't answer me. Instead, he went back through the gate and down the water ground. I didn't see him come back again. Now if he had spoken, it wouldn't have worried me. Mind, he could have been deaf. I later mentioned the matter to Maurice Atkinson at Clove Lodge in case he had seen someone lurking about.

The only other times I felt uneasy happened when there was unusual activity in Baldersdale during the dead of night. Sometimes there would be car headlights coming up the dale — there is no road through, it just peters out alongside the reservoir ground. Fortunately,

Low Birk Hatt is not visible from the road on the north side and I suppose they were just courting couples going to the old quarry. But one did wonder.

Then there were the young men, army cadets I believe, who would appear at odd times of night. If I was still outside, and I did work some funny hours, I would go in and lock the door. I realise they were probably on some legitimate training exercise, but youngsters can be tempted to play tricks.

I was asked more than once at those "Evenings With" whether or not I had thought of acquiring a gun for protection, to which I replied that I would likely have ended up accidentally shooting myself!

The Pleasures and Problems of Visitors

It's not as bad now, but the number of people who have turned up at my door is considerable. Now I do like visitors, and some have become lasting friends. Indeed, one of them became my best friend. She did write in advance to let me know she was coming, but I never got the letter opened.

Sometimes it can be inconvenient, such as when I am rushing to get ready to go somewhere. Or when I am in the middle of a meal — I am a slow eater and like to sit quietly in a corner without being disturbed.

They arrive from all over the place, sometimes in large groups. I've had two coachloads from Ireland, and even one from New Zealand. The organiser of the latter party placed me on the official itinerary of his United Kingdom tour, arranged after several telephone calls from New Zealand with a somewhat amazed Barry Cockcroft. Goodness knows what they must have cost.

There have been a couple from Tasmania and another from Arizona, both of whom invited me to visit them in their homes, and more nice people from Canada where they have formed a group which keeps an eye open for my programmes when they are due for transmission over there and telephone around with the information.

They are the ones that spring to mind, and all were welcome. One who, perhaps, didn't fall into that category was the man who turned up at my door one day, obviously the worse for drink. But even he may have been all right sober!

I am not anti-social, but I think I would rather work with animals than people.

The Ageing Process
. . . and Another Look in the Mirror

I am well into my seventies now, and I find the ageing process an irksome business. You have to take care to put a warm coat on and cover your head most times or inevitably risk after effects. Then there are the pills you need to take regularly to keep things ticking over properly.

And it isn't very comforting when I look in that mirror these days.

But I'm not complaining since I have been blessed with reasonably good health — maybe better in later life than before. If the Good Lord would permit it, I think we shouldn't age beyond fifty . . . staying alive at that point, and in fine physical order!

The Manor House at Bowes

I am descended from some sturdy Dales farming families as my full name — Hannah Bayles Tallentire Hauxwell — indicates. The Bayles were on my father's side whilst mother was born a Tallentire, and they all took their living from the land.

However, there was an exception to this rule if you go back one generation on my mother's side. Her mother came from a different background altogether. She was a Sayer, and was brought up at the Manor House at Bowes, one of the principal houses in the village. They owned a temperance hotel in the area and Grandma Sayer had a bachelor brother who was said to be in the tea business in London. So I think there must have been a bit of money in the family, certainly not short of a bob or two, as they say.

Grandma became a Tallentire when she married Grandad William Tallentire and they set up home in a farm at North Side, Bowes. When you think about it, you have to pity her giving up the privileges of life in a grand house, maybe even servants, to be a farmer's wife. And then to have to cope with so many children — seven, including my mother. Grandad Tallentire was a happy little man, very keen on music and a talented player. It was from him that Mother must have inherited her musical ability.

Because she died when I was young I didn't really get to know Grandma Tallentire so I missed the chance of hearing about life in the Manor House. But Mother talked about it quite a lot. She visited occasionally and was always kindly received.

I went there myself the odd time, sometimes going by bicycle, and even stayed there overnight once during the last war. I remember the occasion very well indeed.

By that time, ownership had passed to Mother's cousin, Margaret Eleanor, born a Sayer then becoming Mrs Robertson. She was a fine lady who liked nice clothes and kept the place in beautiful order, even though it was wartime and hired help for the household was just as scarce as everything else. Those men who could be spared from the land were away serving in the armed forces and women were also busy with work essential to the war effort.

She even had soldiers billeted in what I presume was the old servants' quarters, reached by a back staircase leading from the kitchen, which was very large. It had flag floors, a big black cooking range, a grandfather clock in the corner, three tables, tall windows with shutters and copper pans on display. From there you went through a door into a passage which had an alcove with a window on the right, which may have been a butler's pantry in days gone by. Then you came to the breakfast room which had two windows and led into a long dining room with two doors. Steps then took you into the front hall, which had a cloakroom with a marble washbasin and toilet, and the drawing room was on the right. You could have rolled up the carpets and held a modest ball in either dining or drawing room.

Upstairs was just as splendid, and there were views of the gardens, fields and the village from the windows. Mrs Robertson kindly showed me Grandma's old bedroom. I stayed in a room up the little stairs from the kitchen and she looked after me very well. I recall she cooked an apple pie for me in the big range.

It was such a grand place — still is, of course — and once even had a small farm attached. I am very fond of nice houses, large and small, and if I was very, very rich would make it my business to own several!

Recently, I made a sentimental journey back to the Manor House, and met the present owners who were very pleasant to me. But it turned out to be a bitter-sweet experience. It was the same when a couple of years ago I went to South Stainmoor where my parents were raised and visited the chapel my mother attended.

On both occasions I had such a strange feeling.

The Plague of 1918

The recent 'flu epidemic in this country was serious enough, with hospitals hardly able to cope with the pressure and thousands of people laid low for weeks on end. But it didn't compare with the great 'flu epidemic of 1918.

It took a dreadful toll of my mother's family.

Apparently, it was a worldwide affliction and millions died. I heard it referred to on a radio programme quite recently. The First World War was entering its final stages when it struck and it killed more American soldiers than the Germans. Many schools in Britain had to close and there were more than two thousand deaths in London alone in one week. Although it happened eight years before I was born it was still being talked about when I grew up. I heard that people had been weakened by wartime food restrictions — the quality of flour was particularly poor, and money was scarce.

Usually, it's the elderly who are more at risk in a situation like that, but in the case of my mother's family it was the younger ones who suffered most. She lost two sisters and a brother, all around the same time.

Grandad Hauxwell called it a plague.

At the time of the epidemic, Mother was being brought up by her Uncle Richard Tallentire and Aunt

113

Bessie in South Stainmoor. They had lost their little son and since her mother, Grandma Tallentire, had given birth very quickly to seven children — five daughters and two sons — and her health had been rather fragile, it was considered a suitable arrangement in the circumstances for Mother to live with them. That was how she met my father, who was helping his Uncle Isaac Bayles just over the hill at North Stainmoor.

Mother was sent word that her sister, Maggie, had died from the 'flu. She travelled by train to attend the funeral and when she arrived at Bowes station she was told that her brother, Isaac Thomas, was also dead. It must have been a terrible moment. Apparently, it happened so quickly — Isaac Thomas had been well enough to help out at Spittal Chapel not long before he succumbed. Not long after, another sister, Sarah, died, too. Grandma Tallentire was so ill herself when that happened that she couldn't be told less the shock had fatal consequences. I think she missed the funeral. At least Mother, her sisters Violet and Mary Anne, escaped it. So did her brother, Richard, the youngest of the seven, who was away in France serving in the army.

All the communities around these parts were badly affected. Of course, doctors didn't have much with which to fight the epidemic. But over on the Stainmoor side where Mother and Father lived there was a wonderful man called Doctor Bainbridge who worked night and day to save his 'flu patients. He drove round the area in his car and worked without pause. When he could, he snatched a few hours sleep in the back seat. I understand that he either lost none, or just one of his patients.

Even those who survived suffered the consequences. Mother's sister, Mary Anne, had a baby son who developed a disability (which he bravely disregarded), thought to have been caused by that awful epidemic.

Tea . . . and Television Commercials

It's no secret that I am addicted to tea, and I suppose a higher than average proportion of my weekly household expenditure is spent on it. Oddly, a few years ago I was offered a very substantial sum, indeed, to appear in a television commercial for tea. And it happened to be a brand that I use.

Apparently, I wouldn't have had to say anything, just sit in a particularly well-known Yorkshire café and drink a cup of their tea.

I turned down the offer. At the time I reasoned that when my television programmes are screened people know in advance and can choose whether or not to watch. The same principle applies to my books. Television commercials are different — they catch you unawares. There is no real choice.

I suppose, on reflection, that there is nothing seriously wrong with it and there are some nice people advertising products. I enjoyed Nanette Newman's Fairy Liquid commercial, and Maureen Lipman playing Beattie for British Telecom. I met Maureen when we did a book signing session together and liked her.

116

So television commercials with a sense of humour and catchy tunes can appeal to me, but I do not see the point of some of the more recent crop. Sometimes you cannot even work out just what they are advertising.

If another offer came my way, I'm not sure what I would do. I still lean a little to the opinion that they can be intrusive.

A Little Drop of
What You Fancy . . .

So . . . tea is my tipple, and it is also well-known to anyone who has seen me on television or read the books that I avoid alcoholic beverages. One of my grand-fathers, a truly dear man, was a little too fond of drink and I feared it may run in the family if given a chance to get hold. As I've said, I'm daft enough sober.

There was a pub in Baldersdale when the community was big enough to support one, called the Strathmore Arms. Sometimes during haytime when I was young, I'd be sent to the Strathmore to fetch baccy for my uncle, and be allowed to buy chocolate for myself.

But apart from a liking for rum sauce with Christmas pudding and rum and butter toffee (and being obliged to wet my lips with champagne when persuaded by a charming man in Paris whilst filming the "Innocent Abroad" series, which doesn't really count), I could honestly say that strong drink and I were total strangers.

Until recently.

There is a friend of mine who has set me on the downward path. She makes sloe gin. And I like it. But I restrict it to a sip from a finger glass when I visit.

The Techniques of Interviewing

I've lost count of how many times I have been interviewed, either on television and radio shows or during the "Evenings With". Or how many interviewers with whom I have come face to face.

They do vary, and there have been problems. For me, a good interview is neither more nor less than a good conversation. I don't want to know in advance what people are going to ask me, and if I don't want to answer I reserve the right not to do so. But I have a job sometimes to get the message through. They come to see me before the recording and start to ask questions. I said to one young lady: "Are these the questions you propose to ask me on the programme?", and when she said they were I told her I didn't want to know and to please leave it. As far as I am concerned, once a question has been asked and answered, it's dead.

Now maybe there are people cleverer than me, and trained professionals like actors and actresses, who prefer to rehearse and are capable of putting it over as fresh as a daisy.

Generally, I have been very lucky and can point to some who are very skilled at the art, for art it is. Terry

Wogan springs to mind, of course, and those other lovely Irishmen with television shows in Belfast and Dublin. And my friend Alan Titchmarsh must be included.

I have appeared with Mr Wogan on two occasions, and he just comes round to say a brief hello before the start. Nothing more.

It is also important that the interviewer has the ability to create a spark between him and the interviewee, and persuade his subject to take a liking to him or her all in the space of a couple of minutes. Only the best can do that.

Is It Football or Cricket, Mr Trueman?

I have been privileged to meet a number of famous folk since television brought me to the attention of the public, but not all have been familiar to me. It has not always been possible for me to keep up with current affairs and who's who in the news.

Take Terry Wogan — I had heard him on radio but had never seen him until we came face to face on his television show. And just before he caught me unawares with his big red book, Michael Aspel said to camera that he was worried I would not know who he was or what he was about.

Maybe my most comical meeting with a household name was the day I was introduced to Fred Trueman. He and Barry Cockcroft are old friends, since Barry arranged and directed Fred's early career in television and collaborated on a book. Now I knew that Mr Trueman was a celebrated sportsman, but wasn't sure which sport. As we shook hands, I asked: "Now, is it football or cricket that you play?"

There was a silence, and then everybody burst out laughing, particularly Fred. What a grand person he is.

He explained that cricket was his sport, and later told the story of our meeting on "This Is Your Life" when I was the subject.

Barry said I was probably the only Yorkshire person able to get away with that, because I understand Mr Trueman is known as Fiery Fred.

I do get nervous when I'm talking to an audience. I always say that if you are a singer or a musician and you are not up to standard then you can get by. But if you are talking there is nothing to fall back on.

Glad To Be An Only Child

People do sometimes say to me that being an only child must have been a handicap, that I must have missed having brothers and sisters. Not me. I was glad to be the only one — and still am.

It is a fallacy that all families are very close and supportive. Some are, and are always there for their relatives in times of trouble or need. But there are others that not only fail to give help but also cause resentment and strife.

Many hearts have been broken by those who are close blood relatives.

I'm happy to have avoided that risk. It may be something of a cliché, but it is a great truth that friends you can choose . . . relatives and neighbours you have to put up with what you get!

I hasten to point out that I have mostly been fortunate with neighbours.

I was only seven when my father died. He had been poorly with pernicious anaemia and the doctor said he would never be a robust man again. But he was the main man on the farm and worked on. Then he got pneumonia, and that was it . . .

A Last Word . . . From Walter Dent Bayles

I usually conclude an "Evening With Hannah Hauxwell" by reading a poem, particularly when I am appearing with Barry Cockcroft, who appreciates the rhythm of words as much as me.

So I would like to follow the same pattern with this book, in the sincere hope that you have enjoyed an hour or two in my company.

I once said that in years to come, if you see a ghost walking the pastures of Low Birk Hatt you can be sure it will be me. Now there are several talented Teesdale poets who can fluently reflect these feelings I nurture for the place of my birth, and I read and admire them all. But if I have to select one example from all their work, it would be from the pen of the one who, as mentioned earlier, may be a distant relative of mine. I really identify with his sentiments.

Walter Dent Bayles.

It is from his one published volume, *Pleasures and Treasures of Teesdale*, and is entitled "Beautiful Teesdale — A Tribute".

124

Beautiful Teesdale, I thee adore,
My richest blessings on thee I'd pour.
Oh how I love thee, Dale of my heart,
Life would be empty if we had to part.

Fairest of treasure, from God's Divine Hand,
Wast thou transplanted from His Holy Land?
Pen cannot picture, words cannot tell,
Of all thy beauty, I know so well.

Cascading waterfalls, pine-scented breeze,
Heather clad moorlands, murmuring Tees,
Rare, tinted gentian, delicate rose.
All these delights, wherever one goes.

Rich verdant valleys, lone silent hills,
Tempered by music from soft rippling rills.
'Tis here that I wander from trouble and care,
To the home of the curlew, and slumbering hare.

If time compels me further to roam,
Ne'er I'll forget my wee cottage home.
Though life may take me just where it will,
Memories of Teesdale my soul shall fill.

Then when my earthly travels are o'er,
And I have reached that ethereal shore.
I'll ask the Master, gentle and kind,
If lovely Teesdale still I should find.

Acknowledgements

I offer grateful thanks to Mrs Walter Dent Bayles for her kind permission to use extracts from her husband's wonderful poetry; to my quarter cousin Jack Robinson, another poet of distinction, for the same favour; to Jim McTaggart of the *Teesdale Mercury*, Kathleen Teward, David Joy, Vivien Green and all the friends who have supported me down the years.

Hannah Hauxwell

ISIS publish a wide range of books in large print, from fiction to biography. A full list of titles is available free of charge from the address below. Alternatively, contact your local library for details of their collection of ISIS large print books.

Details of ISIS complete and unabridged audio books are also available.

Any suggestions for books you would like to see in large print or audio are always welcome.

7 Centremead
Osney Mead
Oxford OX2 0ES
(01865) 250333